M000316101

can you make it to the fence?

Coconut Avenue, Inc. - Suggested Retail Prices

Seven Letters That Saved My Life – Seven Principles That Made it Happen
By Dottie Lessard

Hardcover ISBN: 978-0-98010-400-4
Hardcover List Price: $23.95 USD
E-Book ISBN: 978-0-98010-401-1
E-Book List Price: $19.99 USD
Kindle ISBN: 978-0-98010-402-8
Kindle List Price: $9.99 USD
Trade Paper ISBN: 978-0-98010-403-5
Trade Paper List Price: $19.95 USD

Publisher's prices higher in other countries.

For current pricing information, please visit
Coconut Avenue, Inc. on-line:coconutavenue.com

PRAISE FOR

Seven Letters That Saved My Life

"*Dottie Lessard is living proof that dreams, desire, and determination can overcome any adversity and achieve any goal. Internalize her inspiring message and you will realize your own success, regardless of the odds. Truly an amazing guidebook for each of us!*"

-Dr. Denis Waitley, Best-Selling Author of *The Psychology of Winning*

"*Dottie is a firecracker! Her unbridled enthusiasm and unwavering resolve are an inspiration to us all about living authentically. This book is an important reminder that sometimes simply putting one foot in front of the other can be more powerful and empowering than asking ourselves why. If you're looking for motivation and guidance on how to live your life on your own terms,* Seven Letters That Saved My Life, *will give you the boost you need.*"

-Susan Hartman, Associate Publisher/Marketing, *Runner's World*

"*When I think of Dottie I think of fire. Powerful, amazing to look at, and full of unstoppable energy. Having two girls with cystic fibrosis I am grateful to her for inspiring me (us) with her story and determination to keep going no matter what, to live a normal life, and to make a mark in this world. As a news reporter in Detroit I have interviewed many people, politicians, one president, many presidential candidates, rock stars, actors, all sorts of people. More than any of the well-known people I have met, Dottie inspires. Dottie moves people to think, to continue on, to believe in a future, a cure. Dottie has touched our lives, and I'm certain she will inspire you with her new book.*"

-Laura Bonnell, WJR Radio News Reporter, Detroit, Michigan

"Dottie Lessard is an inspiration. She exemplifies the best of what transplant athletics is all about-striving for excellence despite great challenges, motivating others to reach their personal best and showcasing her success story of transplantation. Her new book will motivate you."

-Ellie Schlam, Director of External Communications, National Kidney Foundation, Organizers of the U.S. Transplant Games

"Runners are a special breed. But even in a community of inspiring, can-do people, Dottie Lessard stands out. She is simply one of the strongest, most optimistic people I've ever met. Her life is an against-all-odds success story, and her new book will permanently alter your perceptions of what is possible!"

-David Willey, Editor-in-Chief, *Runner's World*, and President, *American Society of Magazine Editors*

"This is a book of universal principles, applied, lived, and demonstrated through the life of this amazing woman! Using the principles inside, anyone can pursue and become whatever it is that they desire. In Dottie's case, she chose to use the seven letters and seven principles to become a professional athlete. However, these same seven letters and principles can be applied to anything that a person makes a decision to be, do, or achieve."

-Ben Brownsberger, Life Visionary, Elite Coach, and Trainer, ARP Wave Specialist

"I met Dottie in 2006, shortly after she had received a Heroes of Running award from Runner's World magazine. Her story was amazing-a story of triumph over adversity, passion for sport, and a belief that hard work could literally make miracles happen. But Dottie's story really only starts there. Yes, she's beat cystic fibrosis (CF) and survived a double lung transplant to become a successful athlete. Instead of resting easy, she's re-focused her energy on helping others through her coaching and her role as an ambassador for those effected by CF. This book tells both those stories and will inspire anyone who strives to make the world a better place."

-Melanie Strong, *Nike Running*

"There's a reason she calls herself 'the phoenix girl.' Dottie Lessard is living proof that you can die and rise again: wiser, better, and stronger than ever. Once upon a time, she sat on the sidelines, struggling to breathe while all the children in her neighborhood skipped, ran, and played with the kind of wild abandon only children can muster. A quiet voice inside her kept saying, hold on. And she did. A three-time transplant survivor, Dottie now runs with the wind in her hair, buoyed by the lungs of a mountain climber who lost his life and gave her the ability to breathe again. She is my friend and my favorite athlete. Most of all, Dottie Lessard is living proof that if you hold fast to your dreams and just keep putting one foot in front of the other, you'll get to where you want to go. I say: "Run, Dottie, Run!""

-Candy O'Terry, Creator and Co-host of the award-winning radio program *Exceptional Women*, Magic 106.7/Boston

Seven Letters That Saved My Life®

SEVEN PRINCIPLES THAT MADE IT HAPPEN

DOTTIE LESSARD

dottielessard.com

Coconut Avenue®
Chicago, Illinois USA

The Creative Avenue for Best Selling Authors®

Copyright © 2009 by Dottie Lessard. All rights reserved.

Published in the United States by:
Coconut Avenue, Inc. - coconutavenue.com

Editorial Supervisor: Ginny Voedisch
Cover and Interior Design: Nicole Eckenrode
Cover Photograph: James Stewart

The author and the publisher of this book do not dispense any medical advice or psychological advice or prescribe any technique as a form of treatment or a prescription for any physical, mental or emotional conditions. If you suffer from any physical, mental or emotional condition, please consult the proper medical professional for treatment. The intent of this book is not to offer any professional advice of any kind.

The intent of the author and this book is to only offer information of a general nature to assist you in your quest for motivation and personal empowerment. In the event that you use any of the information in this book for yourself, you do so at your own risk and the author and the publisher assume no responsibility for your actions whatsoever.

No part of this book may be produced by any mechanical, photographic, or electronic process, or in the form of a phonographic or video recording; and it may not be used in any retrieval system, transmitted, or otherwise copied for public or private use, other than under the "fair use" provisions of copyright law as brief quotations embodied in articles and reviews, without prior written permission of the publisher.

Trade paper ISBN: 978-0-98010-403-5
Trade paper 1st Edition, October 2010 – Printed in the United States of America

Coconut Avenue®, *The Creative Avenue For Best Selling Authors*®, the Cocount Avenue graphic® and *Seven Letters That Saved My Life*® are registered U.S. Trademarks® of Coconut Avenue, Inc. Trade paper cover copyright © 2010 by Coconut Avenue, Inc. All rights reserved.

TABLE OF CONTENTS

DEDICATION

———

This book is dedicated to my son, Liam, for whom I will forever fight to take breath. My true purpose, my reason for everything, and why I am here. Thank you for being my son. I'll love you forever, you are always in my heart, Momma.

ACKNOWLEDGEMENTS

————

The stories in this book would never have been able to be told without the love and support of so many. I thank everyone who has been a part of my life, for you have touched it, and, in many ways, helped me to be here in this moment. Thank you all, here and in Heaven, so very much.

Thank you for being there this last year through this "awakening" and "journey." Your support and belief in me has meant more than I could ever say.

To Coconut Avenue, Inc., thank you for publishing my manuscript. I am so proud to be one of your authors. You were just what I have been waiting for.

To Polly Bauer and Jackie Walker, thank you for teaching me not only what my voice and story can do but also gifting me with your friendship and bond as successful, confident women. We are often known by the company we keep, and I will be in your company anytime.

To my OPC and EvoSport kids, thank you for your inspiration, time, and laughter through this time of change and growth. I hope the words on these pages are words I will continue to speak to you-never stop believing in your dreams and thanks for being "true."

To Denis Thompson and Jay Schroeder of ARPWave, thank you for your knowledge, vision, and caring to assist me in beating the odds in training and, most importantly, life.

To Dr. Denis Waitley, you have been and will continue to be a source of inspiration for me and a constant reminder that true mentors do exist.

To Cheri Blauwet, for teaching me that I do not stand alone. You are one of my favorite athletes in the whole world. Your courage, determination, strength, passion, and your inner and outer beauty affect all those who meet you.

To Lauryn Williams, you are a true inspiration on and off the track. Your loyalty and commitment to those you love is admirable.

To Donna (Momma) Williams, for adopting me from the start. I cherish our laughter together and your nuggets of pure wisdom. You are a unique star.

To Sharlie Ross Kaltenbach, for truly living with cystic fibrosis. Your steadfast determination, courage, and positive attitude are my fuel. I look forward to both of us dancing with our sons at their weddings.

To everyone at Nike, *Runner's World*, HBO Real Sports, and all my media friends back home in Boston who have never stopped believing in me. It was one or two words from you that allowed me to start writing again, pick myself up after a fall, and believe my voice is worth hearing.

To all the medical staff at Children's Hospital, Mass General, and New England Medical of Boston who have touched my life-my doctors, nurses, pts, blood techs, x-ray techs, transport and housekeeping staff-you have all, in one way or another, helped me to "live."

To everyone who has contributed a quote or testimonial for this book. You are my inspirations, and I am humbled by your willingness to take time for me and give of yourself.

To my family, my true "family," I thank you for always being there. Especially my niece Jenna, Susie B, Al, Dr. Andrew, Linda, and Melissa: thank you for reaching out and being there when it really mattered.

To Linda, thank you for sharing "life," and Melissa, thank you for allowing her to. You are both courageous and giving and I am so proud you are *family*.

To my best friend since age five, Fredia. Thank you for always being the one who believed I could live through anything and for giving me the best childhood memories to share with my audiences.

To my "guardian angels" that like to stay in the quiet background. You have a road to Heaven paved with gold for your generosity in so many ways. Thank you.

To Cathy Savage Fitness and Women's Tri Fitness, you have helped me to live the way I always dreamed. To my coaches Cathy, Jodi, Paula, and Al and my "girls" who helped me run, jump, climb, and fly.

To Lace, thank you for giving me the greatest gift I could ever receive. I will always appreciate your courage and unconditional love. You will always be "our" hero.

To Ryan Hall, for your conviction, strong beliefs, and athleticism. I am proud to be a child of God alongside you.

To Vanessa Underwood, for paving the way for me to not only be a transplant survivor but a transplant thriver.

To Bart (BB) Yasso, the man on the posters I grew up looking at who runs purely for the love of it, the experiences, and the love you share with everyone.

To David Lessard (my dad), for your wisdom many times unspoken but always heard. You are my rock and my foundation. Thank you for being an amazing and caring father and grandfather to Liam.

To Ben, thank you for your knowledge and constant encouragement to remind me that I can be and do anything in life if I never give up working for it and always have hope. You have been a true blessing.

To every child I have had the privilege of meeting and inspiring and all whom I will meet in the future: Never, ever let anyone tell you that you can't because you can, and this is for you.

I love you all,
Dottie

INTRODUCTION

"All your life you are told the things you cannot do. All your life they will say you're not good enough or strong enough or talented enough; they will say you're the wrong height or the wrong weight or the wrong type to play this or be this or achieve this. They will tell you no, a thousand times no, until all the no's become meaningless. All your life they will tell you NO, quite firmly and very quickly. Only you will tell them YES."

-Nike

(Copyright © by Nike, Inc./Wieder and Kennedy Reprinted with permission.)

I have always believed that living and existing are two different things. You become what you desire most when you live the life you desire. I chose to *live* the life I desired, one I could only visualize, despite the steep odds against it ever happening. Each of us holds the power within ourselves to make that choice.

I believe I was born lucky. I arrived into this world knowing what I was meant to be. As long as I can remember I wanted to be strong and healthy, fast and fearless. An athlete. Those are the words I feel when I watch an athlete being an athlete. Those seven simple letters, A-T-H-L-E-T-E, saved my life.

The definition of athlete is "a person who is trained or skilled in exercises, sports, or games requiring physical strength, agility, or stamina." I yearned for those qualities. I yearned to be an athlete in the fullest sense of the word.

To me, being an athlete means fighting against any obstacle that life throws my way with a strong body and determined spirit while living life, moving. Athletes play. They breathe deep and use every part of their body when in competition. I love that.

I live for the feeling of being on a track, waiting to sprint. I live for the excitement of placing my foot on the starting line, ready to take off on an obstacle course, climbing a wall and flipping over a cargo net.

I live for my heart pounding and lungs going in and out with air, purely for life. I get to do all these things by being an athlete. My lifelong desire to be an athlete has saved my life.

You see with the odds I was given, I needed something to get me through, to cause me to fight for something, believe in something I wanted so badly. I would do anything possible to make it happen. I was blessed to be born with the heart of an athlete and the determination to become one.

I came into the world in 1966 six weeks early, fighting, kicking, screaming, and literally backwards! Six weeks later I was diagnosed with cystic fibrosis (CF), a genetic disease that mainly affects the lungs, pancreas, and digestive system.

Back then, CF was more or less a death sentence, especially if you were already showing symptoms. Those who live with CF produce a thick and sticky mucus that causes infections and scarring in the lungs. CF also blocks enzymes that help to digest food. Therefore, CF patients can only absorb about 50% of the nutrients they take in. We need enzyme pills to help us digest our food properly, and most of us take multiple kinds of medications daily. I was taking 13 pills a day by the time I was four years old.

However, I was lucky that I didn't show as many symptoms as others when I was born. My disease progressed rather slowly with blessings, luck, and the hard work I put into fighting and challenging it. I knew that I just wanted to live and live life as long and as fully as I could.

By 1992, CF had started to win. My lungs were failing. I needed to trade them in for some healthier ones or surrender. So I had myself listed on a national organ transplant list, and in October 1994 received a double lung transplant.

Seven years later in 2001, my will and resolve were challenged yet again. After years of medication and post-transplant complications, I was again facing another transplant, this time a kidney. I was lucky and blessed enough to receive a third chance. In October 2002, I underwent a successful kidney transplant.

I will always have challenges. I will probably always be on some sort of anti-rejection medications. Nonetheless, I celebrate the life that I have been given and have made the most of through the powerful principles outlined in this book.

It is my wish that these principles along with my words and stories inspire you to take whatever measures you need to reach your dream, to attain the life you desire. You have the power within you. No one believed I could be a runner or become a professional Nike Athlete, except for me. Believe in yourself and take action, just as I did.

Have you begun your journey toward fulfilling your dream?

If you have, I hope I can give you an extra spark to keep the fire burning.

If you have yet to begin, make this moment, yes, right now, the perfect time to start making your dream a reality.

You can be and do anything. I have, and now it's your turn. So welcome to a little bit of my world, where I didn't take "no" for an answer and now tell them "yes." It is my greatest wish for you to become inspired.

Reach your dream and live life fully. Always!

Dottie
A-T-H-L-E-T-E

HOW TO USE THIS BOOK

———

I start each chapter with one of the seven letters that saved my life, A-T-H-L-E-T-E. Each chapter provides you with a principle corresponding to the letter and an affirmation to say daily to live that principle.

Throughout each chapter I provide you with a number of gifts indicated by the image of a wrapped package. These are my personal words of wisdom based on my battle to survive and live life fully. You can "unwrap" these gifts by applying them to your own life's journey in your own way, for your own circumstances.

You'll also see the image of a winged foot. This icon accompanies brief descriptions of my journey toward becoming an athlete. I hope my experiences inspire you to go forward to live your life to its fullest potential.

Placed throughout each chapter you'll also find quotations to give your spirit the courage to soar beyond any obstacle, real or imagined, that limits you.

Finally, each chapter concludes with an exercise for you to complete. This is a chance for you to take an immediate action step for creating a new life for yourself.

A·T·H·L·E·T·E

MY SEVEN LETTERS

A
Aspire to a purpose.

T
Tackle your fears and move forward.

H
Harmony on the inside creates results on the outside.

L
Live an extraordinary life for yourself.

E
Enrich your life by appreciating your own unique gifts.

T
Trust in a higher power.

E
Encourage yourself and others to do great things.

A·T·H·L·E·T·E

MY SEVEN KEY PRINCIPLES

Principle 1.

Attract what you want by having a definite purpose;
begin with the end in mind.

Principle 2.

Transformation occurs through movement.

Principle 3.

Harness the power of your greatest tool,
your mind. Generate change from the inside out.

Principle 4.

Live your life fully each moment. Living your unique purpose
prevents you from becoming one of society's statistics.

Principle 5.

Enjoy every single moment of your life. Be especially
grateful for it and everything that enriches it.

Principle 6.

Tend to your own spiritual foundation on a regular basis.

Principle 7.

Each day is a brand new opportunity
to raise the bar for yourself.

A·T·H·L·E·T·E

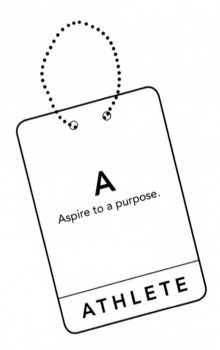

Principle 1.

Attract what you want by having a definite purpose; begin with the end in mind.

"Cherish your visions and your dreams as they are the children of your soul, the blueprints of your ultimate achievements."

-Napoleon Hill

(Copyright © Napoleon Hill Foundation. Reprinted with permission.)

Why am I here? What is my purpose? These are questions virtually all of us have asked. Questions we can only truly answer for ourselves. It's up to each of us to determine what we are here to achieve, what we are here to become, and what we are to have in this life.

Having a definite purpose starts when you make a decision. A decision breathes life into your purpose. A concrete vision materializes as you take continuous and directed action toward a specific end until it is achieved.

Attract what you want by asking for it, believing you can have it, and allowing yourself to receive it. Nurture everything you need to achieve your goal. Always keep your vision of the end result in mind.

AFFIRMATION:

I Am Action Driven for My Purpose.

A
ASPIRE TO A PURPOSE.

You came into this world with your own unique purpose, one that only you can fulfill. You have to aspire to it, no matter what it is. Your purpose may only affect a few or it may change many lives, by finding a cure for a disease or being a teacher. It doesn't matter what it is. It is your purpose and yours alone.

Understanding and discovering your own purpose gives you the green light to succeed. It gives you permission to live your life the way you choose, no matter what anyone else feels or says. Your purpose will bring you joy and contentment, because, when you discover and live it, it radiates from inside of you, touching others. It inspires, it spreads, and it connects.

My purpose was to be an athlete, even though I was born with cystic fibrosis (CF), a chronic and debilitating lung disease. I lived my purpose every waking moment by making my body and mind as strong as possible.

By living my purpose with conviction I was able to disprove survival statistics and everyone who said I wouldn't make it. I overcame my limitations and disregarded anything that was not part of my goal.

Living by your own unique purpose fuels the human gas tank that propels you forward, no matter what is happening in your life. If you look deep enough inside, you will discover your purpose. It is a fundamental part of your core being. Look where your passions lie, your purpose is always nearby. When you find it you will embark on a joyous journey, a course touched by many miracles along the way. Just as you have envisioned it.

You will know when you have discovered your purpose when you achieve a feeling of quiet contentment and peaceful knowing. The point at which you will stop asking "What am I doing?" "Why am I doing it?" or "Why am I here?"

MY RUN TO THE FENCE: MY PURPOSE

I knew at a very young age that my purpose in life was to simply "live"-live fully and live strong. I found out what living was all about in first grade. Every morning I'd arrive at school and head straight to the basketball court. With great excitement I would throw my lunchbox against the crumbling brick wall of the school, line up my sneakers on a painted white line, and wait for a schoolmate to yell "go." When I "went" I felt alive, totally in the moment. I'd dash for about 80 yards toward a shaky rusty fence that surrounded the schoolyard.

I can still remember how amazing it felt to go full force, to defy this thing that lived inside me called CF. Breathing deeply into the lungs that grownups had said were broken, I vowed to myself "I'll show you broken" as I ran straight ahead as fast as I could and slammed right into that fence.

For me the fence was an important symbol. It didn't merely define the school's property. It wasn't simply a barrier. It was a beacon that helped me keep my dreams in sight. It was the goal of an 80-yard dash of deep breaths. As my feet moved fast and my arms pumped, I raced for it with exhilaration and fierce determination.

Once I got there I always smiled. Sometimes my smile felt spiteful, because I knew that I had just accomplished something I was not supposed to be able to do. I wasn't only doing it, I was doing it well, really well.

I knew I was born to run even if I hadn't been born with the lungs to do it. I was born with the heart and mind to do it. That was more than enough.

By third grade, CF had made those early morning races harder and harder. It was more difficult to draw enough air into my lungs as I raced across the playground. Now I had to fight not to be last. Instead of banging into the fence, I reached for it and held on to it for dear life as I tried to catch my breath. Once there I still had a big grin. The joy was still there but running now became more of a struggle.

My efforts often left me with bad headaches that lasted until lunch, sometimes all day. Despite the discomfort, I played at recess in whatever way I could. Playing helped me to remember I was alive.

By the middle of third grade, I had to stop those races

to the fence because I couldn't recover well enough for the school day. But I never truly stopped. Many days for the next two years, and even years later, I would go to the fence and touch it, just to make contact once again. When I was especially motivated, I would bump into it to reclaim that feeling of making impact at full force, every cell in my body screaming to remind me that I was alive.

I never stopped thinking about when I would be able to race through a field, run through the world with deep breaths and a strong body. And, if I felt like slamming into that fence one day, I would and could.

That fence helped me define my purpose: to run through the world one day as an athlete. That was my purpose, and it still is.

MY ARMOR: DRESSING LIKE AN ATHLETE

Easter shoes, white patent leather. Nope, not for me! Nike running shoes for me thank you-blue ones with a white swoosh, light blue with a yellow one, red with orange. Nikes were my dress, play, and school shoes. They were integral in helping me create my end picture of being an athlete. All athletes are strong and healthy, and therefore I believed that if I looked like one I would feel like one. The shoes made me feel strong and healthy even though I wasn't.

I lived 27 years of my life with lungs that wouldn't allow me to run or play sports the way I yearned. Even if I were not yet running or playing in the game, I saw and I lived my end picture every time I walked by a mirror dressed like an athlete.

Every time I laced up my Nikes, they became my badge of honor. That swoosh became a shield I wore to protect my dreams, held inside a chest with lungs that were born tired. Wearing on the outside what I wanted on the inside allowed me to hold on to what I was to be.

When I looked in the mirror, I saw an athlete. I also saw it in other people's eyes. I perceived looks of admiration and respect, not pity or sorrow. Perhaps I had merely seen what I wanted, but I believed it. I witnessed my end picture through my eyes and theirs. Decked out in my Nikes and a tracksuit, I was the athlete I was born to be.

BECOMING STRONG: I BUILT MY BODY FOR BATTLE

In early 1992 my case was reviewed for the transplant list by the medical team at Massachusetts General Hospital (Mass General). When the transplant doctors first looked at my medical file, they thought they had the wrong MRI scans. "Ms. Lessard has too much muscle mass to be an acceptable candidate for a lung transplant," they concluded. But my CF doctor, Dr. Khaw spoke up. "No, that's Dottie. She works out all the time."

At that point, they began to pay a little extra attention to me. My dedication to keeping myself as fit as possible while waiting for the transplant paid off. The doctors had expected a lot less muscle mass and a lot more fatty tissue from inactivity. But after reviewing my lung function tests, they saw that my lungs were indeed severely impaired. They were amazed that I wasn't on constant oxygen. It appeared that through daily exercise and training my body had adapted to what little oxygen it received.

I will always believe that knowing my unique purpose and owning it helped keep my body going. I also received a great deal of support from my parents, who never wavered. They were there every moment, making meals or protein shakes when I was really sick, when I had to decide whether to breathe or chew.

I stressed and pushed my body daily to do things it didn't want to and wasn't supposed to do. Yet, my body found ways to meet my demands because I didn't give up asking of it. No matter how bad the headaches were or how many breaks I needed to take, I kept pushing.

You see, I truly believe things can be changed if you work hard to fully live your purpose. I concentrated on what I could control and ignored what I couldn't. I took action and built my body into a finely tuned machine so that my body would be ready and worthy to receive the gift of new lungs.

I was self-made, strong.

*I wanted my body to be a Ferrari not a beat-up, broken-down jalopy.
It was a sleek machine just waiting for replacement parts. Every
day I would walk on the treadmill, lift weights, ride my bike, or hit
a punching bag. I was preparing for the future I was going to have.
Everyone can do something daily to achieve one's purpose, no matter
what the situation. The littlest things can and do make a difference.
Believe in yourself and take the first step, determine your purpose.
Who cares how little it is or how funny it looks? If it is going to bring
you the outcome you desire, you just do it, period.*

TAKING MY CHANCE: CALLING MY OWN ODDS

When I first talked to Dr. Khaw in 1991 and told him I wanted
to be placed on the transplant list, he told me I wasn't ready.
His exact words were, "You aren't sick enough yet." He wasn't
completely sold on this transplant thing yet, but I knew better.

Some of first double lung transplants ever performed on
CF patients had been done only a few years before. My friend
Betty was one of the first recipients of a double lung transplant
at Mass General due to CF. She was a true inspiration. Here
she was raising a family and living with CF. I was inspired by
her recovery from surgery, too. Just a week before I had had
the transplant conversation with Dr. Khaw, I was amazed to see
Betty laugh without breaking into a coughing fit.

Dr. Khaw cautioned me that the operation wasn't a cure. Undaunted I replied, "I know, but I want to live not just exist. That's what I'm doing now. I am sick of spending most of my time in a hospital and not being able to breathe. I want to start the transplant workup, please." He said he would think about it. I was relentless. I pestered him for six months. I drove him crazy with my endless requests. Finally, he agreed to meet with the transplant team.

Dr. Khaw told the team that he considered me a rare case but admitted that he didn't think I was quite ready. At that time people were put on the transplant list when they no longer had a choice. My lungs were getting by, and I could've waited. I didn't want to.

I wanted to begin my battle as soon as possible so I would have enough left of me to live life as I had intended. I also thought that it would be better to "trade in" sick lungs that still worked a little rather than ones that didn't function at all. I wanted to bring as much as I could to "the table."

Finally, during one of my frequent stays at the hospital, I began a series of pre-transplant tests. I was poked, prodded, and evaluated physically and mentally.

"Why do you want to get a lung transplant?" the staff asked. "Because I want to breathe and become an athlete," I replied. "What a stupid question," I said to myself. It was so simple and obvious to me. I was going to be an athlete. Period.

How lucky I would be to get a transplant at my own hospital. Take out the bad lungs and put in good ones. That is what I focused on. Others had not been so fortunate. Penny, my best friend since we were 11, had also had CF and had wanted new lungs. But, back in 1989, there hadn't been many lung transplants performed yet on CF patients. Penny lost her battle and passed away.

When Dr. Khaw suggested I wait for the transplant, I simply didn't hear him. I didn't hear Dr. Ginns, the lung transplant pulmonologist say, "Dottie, you know you are just trading one disease for another. Your chances are 50/50 just to get off the table." I take that back. I did hear Dr. Ginns. I heard him say, "You have a 50% chance of being able to run."

One day a little black thing the size and shape of a matchbox arrived in the mail. It was my transplant beeper-my ticket to a new life! "Beep, beep, beep" it sounded as I took it out of the padded yellow envelope. I examined my new best friend, my light saber, my lucky rabbit's foot.

That beeper stayed by my side for the next two years and seven months. During that time all I could think about was that 50% survival rate and becoming an athlete.

If you constantly visualize what you want and give it emotion, you will begin to believe that you can have it because it has become familiar. It then becomes attainable. Your mind doesn't know it's not yet real.

At first you may have a hard time seeing yourself being, doing, having, or achieving your purpose. Everyone can do something to achieve one's life purpose. The littlest things can and do make a big difference. If you believe it and live it in your mind, no one will be able to take it away from you. You must see what you want. You must believe your purpose is to make your end picture your ultimate wish. Tell yourself every day it will happen. And it will. You do not need to know the how or when or why. Just trust that it will happen. Make your actions the colors that make your life a work of art.

*"To truly live life fully, we must do the things
we believe we cannot."*

This is a statement that I came up with. I repeat it daily.
I live it. This is my legacy. Anyone who has the courage to live
his or her own unique purpose should use it. Do you have the
courage to say it? Do you have the courage to live it?

As I battled CF, I would suit up in Nike running shoes
and a tracksuit. It was my uniform to remind me of my
purpose. It was something real I could feel and touch, every
single day. Now, I get to wear this uniform because I am
officially part of the Nike team, a professional Nike Athlete.

I also used pictures. Pictures were things I could look at,
touch, and feel daily. Here is a copy of a picture I drew to look
at while waiting for my new lungs. This picture made me an
athlete. It allowed me to aspire to my unique purpose.

This picture looks a lot like the photo of me on the
back cover of this book. An actual Nike girl!

(The phrase "Nike Girl" used with permission.)

(Copyright © 1993 by Dottie Lessard. All rights reserved.)

Talk about an end picture coming true! If I was able to give life and color to my purpose when my health was so broken, when I didn't yet have new lungs or a new kidney, what can you do?

YOUR TURN:

Determine your purpose!

———————

Get out your colored pencils, crayons, or paints and start coloring in the box on the next page to define your purpose. When you are finished, place your picture somewhere you can see it every day.

Give it life, breathe your feeling and emotions into it. Live the colors you selected with your actions, with every breath you take. You can achieve it. I did.

I ASPIRE TO MY OWN UNIQUE PURPOSE.

A·T·H·L·E·T·E

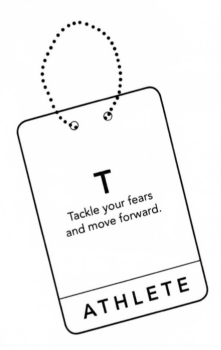

T

Tackle your fears
and move forward.

ATHLETE

Principle 2.

Transformation occurs through movement.

"Movement is the key to life. If you are not moving forward you are accelerating the death process."

-Jay Schroeder, elite coach and developer of
EvoSport and UltraFit Training

Moving and being active are the keys to living life fully and achieving your purpose. You must decide to keep going, especially when you think you can't go any further, achieve any more, take one more breath, take one more step, or do one more thing.

To stop moving and become inactive is the quickest way to go from living a full, happy, and passionate life to merely existing.

To move is to take charge of your destiny. Movement is reclaiming your own power. Movement is the key to allowing yourself to live.

AFFIRMATION:

I Am Thankful for My Ability to Move.

T

TACKLE YOUR FEARS AND MOVE FORWARD.

As long as you are moving, you are going to achieve your purpose. The speed or distance does not matter, especially when moving or not can mean the difference between life and death. If you truly think about it, life is a series of choices, sometimes as simple as whether to breathe or not.

Movement is life. Stop moving and the death of a goal, dream, or desire occurs very quickly. When you choose to move, you take action; you make a choice to improve your life. Life needs to be lived. It needs to be felt, experienced, touched, and celebrated. Life is lived through movement.

I believe that when you experience pain, it is an indication that something in your life needs to change. When you face obstacles in life, just start moving and you will make progress physically and mentally. You overcome obstacles through movement.

"I guess living and existing are two different things to me. I'm just not happy sitting on the couch watching TV. I need to be out, experiencing life, feeling life…and feeling life to me is sprinting up the hills gasping for breath." That was what I said while I was interviewed for a television documentary called Ironwoman, filmed by HBO Real Sports. Ask yourself right now are you living or existing?

Everything in life is in constant motion... When water flows it possesses great beauty and power to cause change. Now think of water as it sits still. It gets mucky and dirty. Since our bodies are comprised of mostly water, we need to let it flow, move it, all of it, don't allow yourself to get mucky...ever.

LET ME PLAY: CHOOSING TO MOVE

Even though the disease in my lungs became more obvious over time, the first signs of CF were asthmatic, a tightening of the airways especially with exertion. Around age 10, I began to develop "green stuff," a code word we with CF use for an infection in the lungs. Yet, I still found a way to live my life without placing limitations on myself. I made a decision to tell CF that it couldn't control me and keep me from moving.

I knew my CF lungs were all I had to work with, but I never allowed them to discourage me even when they screamed "stop!" I walked fast, laughed, and, at times, simply just moved. But in order to do that I had to figure out how to deal with what I had been given.

Sometimes when I played sports it would feel as if there were rubber bands wound around my lungs. However, after moving around a bit and enduring a few coughing fits, which I would discreetly have behind a tree so no one would see, the "elastic" seemed to stretch.

It was natural for me to want to move, to make my body respond to my wishes. When I was growing up, there were always kids playing outside the apartment complex. I wanted to be one of them and worked hard at always trying to keep up with them.

Every Sunday after church, I would head over to the basketball court. I would shoot the ball from all different areas of the court. I became a great shot. If I missed a hoop, I had to endure a penalty: chase the ball all the way down the grassy hill and bring it back up again.

Although this presented a challenge with my impaired breathing, something inside me, some extra part God put inside me as part of my unique purpose, liked the thrill of chasing that ball down the hill. I have come to understand that I have always chased life like that ball, a bit short of breath but with a lot of satisfaction that I was moving.

I also played catch with my dad. I had a really good curve ball as a baseball pitcher. I also had a great spiral as a football quarterback. I practiced what I could control, activities that used the least amount of air. In any game we played, I mastered what I could achieve with a limited lung capacity and what wouldn't bring on a coughing fit that might stop me dead in my tracks.

When I played dodge ball, I was always the most accurate at hitting the other kids. Plus, because I was so skinny, I was a hard target to hit! I was never picked last for any neighborhood game. Never.

Even with bad lungs, kids knew, nine times out of ten, I was the one they could count on to make a basket, strike someone out, or throw a touchdown pass.

So you see I never stopped moving. Through movement, through taking action no matter how measured or small, I had no limits. Even if I just moved my leg, my arm, my body, or my mind. I kept going. I may not have moved as fast or as far as my teammates, but I was on the same team because I mastered what I could.

You wouldn't find me on the sidelines because I couldn't breathe or run fast. I made up for that with a perfect jump shot, pitch, or spiral. Most days my mother would have to come out and literally drag me home off the court or field for supper. Even my mouth seemed to move a lot, too much as my mother often reminded me. Yet, she could see that being stubborn wasn't always a bad thing. Especially when you are trying to live!

We all have some type of limitations in life-personal problems, health issues, financial challenges, etc. These are the rubber bands we place on ourselves. However, if we keep moving, we can stretch them. We can move what limits us one way or another.

FIGHTING BACK: THE POWER OF WORKING OUT

I knew my health was starting to fail, but I also knew I had to keep living. I couldn't let my body think I was giving up on it. I was determined to try as hard as I could to continue moving forward in my life, so I enrolled in fashion design classes at a Boston community college. As much as I wanted desperately to go away to college, I knew, for the time being, I could manage my health better by staying close to home.

I commuted by train three days a week, and during those trips I felt like the world opened up a tiny bit. But once I got to school, my limitations became obvious. Each morning I had to climb four flights of stairs to my first class. Often I missed the first 15 minutes of the lecture trying to get my breath under control.

The constant physical therapy on my chest became more important than ever. I had to do it two times a day for 30 minutes to clear the CF "junk" out of my lungs. Proper nutrition became crucial as frequent infections from CF caused me to lose weight quickly, and I was starting to get short of breath a lot easier. I had to fight harder than ever now to keep moving forward.

Limitations were starting to grow like trees around me. However, I persevered. Movement became my lifeline.

"Movement creates an opportunity to make
a path, a clearing to dance in, to revel in,
and to live life in."

I soon discovered another avenue for movement: lifting weights. When I mentioned my desire to pursue weight training to a guy I was dating, he dismissed it by saying "girls shouldn't lift weights." Did he just say I couldn't/shouldn't do something? He didn't know me at all.

I told my dad I wanted to put a weight bench in the therapy room. Because he knew anything physical would be good for me, he agreed. That very night we went to Sears and purchased a bench and some weights.

I found a new weapon that night. The entire room took on a whole new meaning for me. Instead of it being the place where I was treated for CF, it became the room where I treated my CF. A space where I had power.

"Find a way to treat your own symptoms," I thought. From the moment I sat on the bench, picked up a five-pound weight, and started doing bicep curls, I realized that I had found the key-challenging my muscles. I found a way to move and not be too short of breath, to adapt and still work out and move. Lifting weights would one day open up a door to a whole new world. I felt empowered. I felt alive.

I sat down for most of the weight exercises and took breaks in between sets. I had coughing fits but usually as a conscious effort to clear the junk out of my lungs. I was in control in my weight room. Some nights I would spend a couple of hours doing a workout that was only supposed to take 30 minutes. But I did it, no matter how long it took I lifted weights and moved muscle.

The weight room was my place for release. It became my temple. And believe me I did my fair share of praying in there, too. It's also where I could dance to music, hit the speed bag, and give high fives to posters of pro volleyball player Gabby Reece and Steve Prefontaine (Oregon runner, 1972 Olympian, and considered by many to be the best American distance runner of all time). Both were Nike Athletes. I would be a Nike Athlete too one day. I could see it, feel it, and taste it. I lived life as fully as I could those days by moving in that room.

I did anything I could to be active and stay strong, not just in the physical sense but mentally as well. I was fighting back against something that was slowly taking me away from myself.

Every night at the end of a workout, at the close of a deliberate session of movement, I would whisper defiantly, "Screw you CF, you are NOT going to win!"

RECIPE FOR MOVEMENT:
WATCHING THE WHITE DOT PASS BY

The minute I received my transplant beeper, I was ready to begin intensive training. My drill sergeant was the laminated "Just Do It" sign that hung on the living room wall.

My mother just loved it when people saw it for the first time, the bold black letters and red swoosh hanging next to a beautiful oil painting of a fall New England day. The painting matched the couch and chair. The Nike sign didn't.

That was just fine with her though, because she knew

that that sign was my motivation to keep moving. And I did, although I have to admit that during the last year of waiting for my lung transplant I began to hate walking on the tread-mill. Okay, it was more of a love/hate relationship.

I hated not being able to run as freely as I would have liked, but I loved the way I felt proud when I finished my workout. I was so happy to keep my feet moving at the lightning speed of two miles-per-hour. It didn't matter if on some days I only did a couple minutes at a time instead of continuously for 25 minutes. Either way I was stronger when I stepped off.

I was reminded I was alive every day I made the choice to step onto that treadmill and move. I would lace up my Nikes, put on my headphones, and just walk. "Just do some-thing, Dottie," I would say to myself as I stared at the "Just Do It" sign. I knew I wasn't one of the Nike runners (yet) but I was going to be. It started with one step, one foot in front of the other, making me move.

Within minutes of starting, however, my lungs would remind me they were "special" as I tried to breathe deep down inside for extra air. When I had to step off to the side of the treadmill for a coughing fit, I reminded myself that I was winning against CF because I was clearing out the junk that caused infections and scarring. It was during those challenging moments that I paid extra attention to a white dot on the treadmill belt. I watched it pass underneath my feet over and over again, taking pride each time it came past again. It proved I was moving, however slowly. It gave me strength.

*Life is like a treadmill. If you stop moving, you might get caught
in the treadmill belt. You can always take another step no matter
how bad you think things are. It will help you keep moving in the
right direction toward fulfilling your purpose. Movement is life.
Life is movement. Moving is a shift from existing to living.*

MOVE: EVEN IF IT MEANS GETTING PULLED

In 1994 I finally received my new lungs which allowed me
to begin my new life. Six years later, I was sick again. Yet,
I looked at this new challenge as another opportunity to
move forward.

I needed another transplant. I had been battling high
blood pressure off and on for a year or so, and it went un-
diagnosed for a while because I was so fit. Little did I know
that the high blood pressure was slowly killing my kidneys.

I had a bout of viral meningitis the previous year and
was put on a few different antibiotics. I was also taking anti-
rejection drugs for my new lungs. Both kinds of medication
proved to be very detrimental to my kidneys.

Doctors speculated the combination of all the drugs,
including the immunosuppressive drugs for the transplant,
growing up with CF, and being in and out of the hospital so
many times during the wait for my transplant (I was in for

two weeks every five to six weeks the last year and a half before my transplant) had put a tremendous strain on my kidneys.

For the first time ever the rest of my body was weaker than my lungs were. It was a new sickness, and it was rough. It ran me over like a runaway truck.

I questioned whether I had the right to ask God for another chance at life, to receive, one more time, the ultimate gift one family could give to another. Was I worthy? The only way I could answer that question was to believe that God had put me here to achieve my unique purpose-to survive all this and to continue to be an athlete.

I vowed always to cherish the gift I had received on October 27, 1994, my new lungs, and promised to do likewise if I were blessed enough to receive a kidney. I knew I would devote my life to doing well and making a difference. So a new journey began, another wait, another fight.

My life was slipping away fast, and people were starting to give up on me. I heard the whispers in the hospital hallways, about how sick I was, how I had already lived seven years with a lung transplant and how kidney dialysis was not working.

It was all true. I was pretty damn sick, and it sucked. I was tethered to a dialysis tube every night for 10 hours to clear the toxins out of my system because my kidneys could no longer do it. My creatinine, a protein used to measure kidney function, level remained at the dangerously high level of 10, when normal is between 0.7 and 1.5. Worst of all, after waiting 28 years, I had finally known what it felt like to run, to sprint up a hill only to have that feeling gone again. Just like that.

I was really sick, but I couldn't give up. I guess when God gave me that fighting spirit, he took out the part that allowed me to doubt. I have never known the option of giving up. It might have been tempting to consider it but there wasn't, and still isn't, a part of me able to comprehend giving up. How do you even do that? The answer is, you don't, ever.

I had to keep moving and fight to do the simplest things. Sometimes I would crawl to the bathroom on my hands and knees when no one was home because I refused to use a bedpan.

Many days and nights I would look out the front window of my home at the street I had once jogged on, the hill I once sprinted up. I forced myself to tackle them once again, this time with my mind, visualizing my movements. I was heartbroken that these new lungs that I had earned and cherished were not getting to experience the joy of breathing deeply, in and out, hard and fast, because other parts of my body were too tired.

It was when I felt my heart would stop from sadness that I had to get determined, pull up the courage, and remember what had gotten me through everything else. Inside this tired body, the desire to run still flickered. I had to ignite it with the decision to move, to fight for life, to demand it for myself, and remind my body exactly what life was all about. I reminded my mind, my broken heart, my new lungs, and those worn-out kidneys that I was still here and I could still move.

It's then that I would lace up my Nikes, tying them extra tight. I would wrap my weak hand around my dog Guinness's red leash and let him lead me outside into the sunlight for my daily walk. When I didn't have any strength to do it alone, he would walk me. And I appreciated his help.

I marveled as my feet moved underneath me, passing cracks in the cement. I paid careful attention to the motion of it all, the look of the neighbor's houses, the mailboxes, the trees, and the driveways as I walked past. I was still passing them by, now slower but moving just the same.

No matter how painful those walks were or how tired they left me, I always felt happy. Some sort of happiness arose from the sadness and struggle of being sick again, because I was living life by moving.

I don't care how it is you move, just do it and just start. Move toward your purpose, take action. Nothing in life is meant to come to you. You must move to get it. Don't put pressure on yourself to do a certain amount or make a certain quota, just start, move. Move toward the direction you want your life to go. Making even the tiniest steps will get you closer than if you stayed stationary thinking about it or watching someone else do it. Moving, choosing to do it for yourself will empower you. Be the person you admire by moving. Be the person other people admire by moving.

YOUR TURN:

Tackle your fears by moving!

Whatever is the right action for you to tackle your fears, take the first step. That first step will move you closer to achieving your purpose. Move one step forward. Right now!

HERE ARE SEVEN EXAMPLES THAT I CAME UP WITH TO HELP YOU START MOVING.

1. *Take the stairs instead of the elevator (even if you only take one flight and the elevator the other six).*
2. *Do "commercial workouts" when you are watching television. Walk around your house, up and down the stairs, grab some soup cans and do some arm workouts, get up and down from a kitchen chair during commercial breaks.*
3. *Volunteer at your local animal shelter to walk a dog, or two or three. Or let the dogs walk you.*
4. *Do housework at a fast pace and scrub your floors extra hard.*
5. *Walk around the mall without shopping.*
6. *Find a new active hobby. Share it with a friend.*
7. *Find an activity you are passionate about and find a way to do it. Even if it is only for a couple minutes at first, alone while everyone is asleep in the house. Move even if it seems silly, funny, crooked, or upside down.*

On the next page, create your own list of seven ways in which you are going to tackle your fears and move forward. Remember, no step is too small, even if it moves you forward one inch!

SEVEN THINGS I AM GOING TO DO TO TACKLE
MY FEARS AND MOVE FORWARD:

1.

2.

3.

4.

5.

6.

7.

A·T·H·L·E·T·E

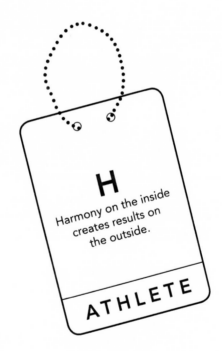

H

Harmony on the inside creates results on the outside.

ATHLETE

Principle 3.

Harness the power of your greatest tool, your mind. Generate change from the inside out.

"I have learned through both my career as a professional athlete and as a physician that the mind and the body are one. One cannot will the body to perform or achieve without complete investment from the mind. The physiologic state of our body, in turn, also controls our mental health, vigor, and energy."

-Cheri Blauwet, M.D.. physician and three-time Paralympian

Your mind and thoughts are very powerful. Think only about what you want, what you desire. Don't think about what you don't want or that's what you will get—what you don't want.

Good thoughts generate good feelings, which generate positive outer results. Remember, your body is an external reflection of your internal thoughts.

AFFIRMATION:

I Hold within My Mind Seeds of Greatness to Grow.

H

HARMONY ON THE INSIDE CREATES RESULTS ON THE OUTSIDE.

No matter what your situation is, you've got to begin using what's on the inside to draw yourself closer to your dreams. When you close your eyes, you have to feel it, hear it, taste it, live it, experience it on the inside every day without fail.

In the process you will start to take actions in your life and attract the results that you seek. The outer results come from the harmony you generate within yourself, something only you can do.

When I was little I occupied my mind with the endpoint
I had set for myself when I grew up, when I could
breathe. I didn't know when that would be, but I just
knew it would happen. I never doubted it. In my mind
I would be an athlete, be strong and run. I believed
nothing else, and no one could tell me differently.

LIVING WITHIN: COMPETE EVERY DAY IN MIND, HEART, AND SOUL

I am not going to lie. It was pretty rough growing up short of breath and even harder waiting for a lung transplant. Once I was listed on the transplant list and got my beeper, I devoted myself to staying as healthy as I could until I received that missing piece of me, new lungs that worked so I could run, jump, hop, or skip. When I was listed, I was told it would take about a year to receive my lung transplant. It took two years and seven months.

I had to do some digging down deep to get to that day. I had to generate the end result I wanted by visualizing it and activating feelings to give it life. My lung capacity had decreased to the point where one lung was operating at 15% of capacity, the other at 20%. That didn't leave me a whole lot of room to play, but I played anyway.

At this point I couldn't use my body the way I wanted to, so I began relying on my greatest tool: my mind. Even though I wasn't actively a runner, I ran every day in my mind.

I never let go of the feeling of running, of slapping into that rusty old fence behind my grammar school. I have thought about that experience many times and even now I can feel my hair flying in the wind as my legs and arms propelled me forward, catching air with joy and excitement. I remember how the ground felt as I sprung from it and how amazing the world looked as it sped by out of the corner of my eye.

When I could no longer physically do my daily workouts, I did them in my mind's eye. I exercised using my thoughts to propel me toward what I would become. Instead of reading about medications, test results, disease updates, I sought knowledge from my world of dreams. I was only interested in learning more about what I would become, what I wanted, not more about what I hated having.

Runner's World magazine was my bible. I loved learning about what it felt like to run, how to train, and injuries to avoid. (OK, sometimes I skipped that section.) I loved reading about how much runners loved what they did. I studied the photographs, amazed at how efficiently their bodies worked and how strong their lungs had to be.

"Wow," I thought. "I cannot wait to run like that." I would picture myself doing it, sometimes attempting stretches and running forms in my socks and pajamas.

I would watch fitness shows and read magazines like *Oxygen* and *Fitness*. Watching the Body Shaping TV show was a daily ritual Monday through Friday. I would study the trainers, admiring how strong they were and how they performed the workouts with little effort. They were athletes, able to do what they loved. I adapted what they did to what I could do at the moment. I made mental notes on what I couldn't do and filed it under "when," because I knew there would be a "when."

I loved watching the Olympics (and still do). Every time track and field was on I would get in my starting position, ready to sprint. I imagined I was on the starting line, my heart racing, lungs fully functioning, and then I was off racing with the Olympic athletes around the track.

I loved the way the sprinters looked, like powerful thoroughbred horses in full gallop. I also enjoyed watching marathons, intrigued by how the runners strategically planned their break-out moment. I loved experiencing the joy they felt when they saw the finish line.

Joan Benoit's gold medal win in the women's marathon in the 1984 Olympics in Los Angeles was like nutrition to my body, oxygen to my lungs. I will never forget watching her on TV and weeping with joy for her and for all of us girls who dreamed of feeling what she was feeling. That memory fueled my mind for a long time and still does, especially when I have to run long and dig deep. Thanks Joanie!

TEMPORARY PATIENT: FULL-TIME ATHLETE

There were many times when I was hospitalized sick as a dog with a bad lung infection, a temperature well over 100 degrees, and extremely short of breath. Although I was always grateful to be there when I was sick-the staff truly took care of me and helped me live-I never ever liked being a patient.

I didn't like to wear a "johnnie" (a hospital gown). I don't like putting on anything backward. OK, there were a few times I actually wore that stupid hospital gown. In fact, I was actually happy to have it on when I was too tired to roll up my sleeves for a blood draw or remove my shirt so that someone could listen to my lungs. When possible though I remained dressed in my clothes, my athlete clothes.

Inside my hospital room was an athlete in a patient's body...always. I even wore New England Patriots football jerseys or Boston Bruin hockey jerseys if I was in the hospital during football or hockey season (Bobby Orr, Ray Bourque and yes, #6, Gord Kluzak). I loved jerseys of all kinds because I could fit my big intravenous needle wrap from my arm or hand under them.

I always walked into the hospital as if it were only going to be a temporary visit. I would play the role of patient only for as long as I needed to. When I got intravenous antibiotics and did chest PT three times a day, I took it like an athlete-after all I was in the game of my life.

I would politely correct anyone who referred to me as a patient. Whenever I was called to go down for tests, the transport person would be surprised to see me sitting in the chair fully dressed. "Are you the patient?" they would venture. I would smile and reply, "No, I'm the athlete. But, yes, I guess I'm the patient for today." Then I would lace up my running shoes instead of putting on the usual patient slippers, which I refused to wear.

My running shoes helped me keep it together as I was being wheeled through dreary, cold, and, from my perspective, sometimes scary hospital hallways. All I needed was to look down at those swooshes on my shoes, happy not to see the required hospital "foamies" stamped "Property of Massachusetts General Hospital."

Most of the transport people liked the change of scenery, too. I may have been a patient going for a painful test, but at least I did it bravely with my end picture in mind. I was always in training, and I would never let what I wanted leave my mind, even if I didn't know when the real game would begin.

Believe it and you can achieve it. Make it familiar, don't let it out of your mind. Don't put your mind to rest at night without affirming your dreams and goals. See what you want before you lay your head down to sleep. When you wake up tell your mind again. Every morning set your goal for the day. Your mind will carry it and nurture it if you allow it to do so. It will take you to your ultimate goal. The mind will listen. Just make sure you are telling it the right things.

READY FOR LIFE AND WORK:
MY AT-HOME CF DEGREE

Making it to this point in my life had a lot to do with being active as a child and doing specific exercises when my lungs really started to decline. I wanted to know all about how I could stay strong and how to teach others to do it, too.

I wanted to feel like I was doing something while waiting for my chance. I knew I needed to keep my eye on the prize, getting to the other side. Not to Heaven, not that other side, but my heaven here, a place where deep breaths came easy and Nike treads got worn out from use.

I knew I wanted to become a certified personal trainer. I couldn't actually train much, but I could learn. I wanted to absorb everything about being a great trainer and be ready to go when my body was healthy.

Back in 1993, I couldn't go online and search the Internet, so I looked in the back of all my fitness and running magazines. I saw a correspondence course through which you could study and take tests via mail and phone to become a certified personal trainer at home.

Perfect, no one would have to know I was studying from bed or from a hospital room hooked up to IVs. I ordered the at-home course and put all my energy into learning about the human body and how to make it, and keep it, strong.

I learned about muscles, lungs, and the heart. I learned about exercises-how to do them and which ones to do for specific muscles. I took a test after each chapter and mailed it in, then waited to see my results. I was excited to get up in the morning and face the ugly first-of-the-day coughing fits, because I knew I was going to school my way and working on my life.

In the hospital, I remember nurses coming in to my room to talk. "I can't chat now, I'm studying," I would say. That felt great. I felt worthy and knew that once I got my lungs I would be ready to inspire others and help them be healthy. I was becoming knowledgeable about my own athletic goals. I was making the most of those long days of waiting. It took me almost a year to get my certification.

By the summer of 1994 I had passed the two-year mark waiting for a new set of lungs, and I was getting tired, really tired, physically and mentally. I just kept focusing my thoughts on what my transplant surgeon Dr. Wain had promised me,

"I will find just the right lungs for you." He knew I was silently hoping for the lungs of a runner or other athlete.

I kept my head in the books, and when I got worried I studied harder. The last few tests were rough because of the headaches I would get from coughing or simply being too tired. But I finished my degree.

Going through all that made the day I received my diploma even more special. I had just been released from the hospital. My lungs had been cleaned out but just six days later I was already feeling "junky." I was starting to get a little nervous about how long I could fight this battle, and I didn't like how CF was working harder and harder to control me.

But then the mailman delivered a large manila envelope with a CF certification emblem on it, I knew what it was. I buzzed with excitement and laughed at the play on words. I had CF, and now I was a CF Trainer, a *Certified Fitness* Trainer. I read the name on the certificate: Dottie Lessard. It was official, I had done it.

I now had a career waiting for me once I could breathe with new pink lungs. I could help others feel healthy and get strong, too.

I always visualized my end point. Taking action on what I could do, using the body parts that did work. I kept myself going and remained in a place of positive thought. I never lost focus of my goal, even though it seemed it was getting harder to reach physically. My mind allowed me to be strengthened from the inside out to stay strong when other body parts were tired out.

Everyone gets tired out in one way or another. We must always keep our minds clear and strong. Change negative thoughts into positive ones. If you believe it in your mind, you can achieve it with your actions.

"I am a dreamer. I always will be.
I HAVE to be!"

You become what you think about most. You can be what you believe you can become. The thoughts you invest with emotions and feelings become magnets that attract what you desire. Make a conscious decision to attract what you want.

Even when my parents first explained to me that it is possible to die from CF, I never ever believed I would.

I collected positive sayings, and kept a scrapbook of dreams inside my heart, my soul, and my mind. I kept actual items signifying my dreams in a Dream Drawer. While I never truly focused on growing up, I never believed I would die either.

I was practicing the Law of Attraction and using visualization techniques without even really knowing it. I was practicing these techniques long before they became popular in books like *The Secret*. I had my own secret, and I just knew intuitively that these were the techniques I needed to use to survive.

I would keep reminders of what I wanted to become in a Dream
Drawer. As far back as I can remember, I had a drawer
filled with dreams of what I wanted to become: an athlete.

My Dream Drawer was my sock drawer. When I was younger I would use it to store tags from athletic clothes with sayings such as "Be a Player" or "Get in the Game." I also kept a used batting glove, because I loved how its worn state showed that I had actually played with it at one time. There were ticket stubs to sporting events, brochures for local races in town, articles on runners from the local paper, words cut out from magazines that were powerful to me, pictures and autographs of athletes, and written goals I never let go of. Anything tangible that I could pull out at different times to remind me what I was living for and going to be, an athlete.

I will now keep this book in the drawer, under my socks along with those meaningful scraps and trinkets. The objects that I store in this special place remind me of where I came from, what I have been through, and that anything is possible if you allow it.

When you take action, believe in yourself, and inspire enough other people, you might be rewarded when you least expect it. In my Dream Drawer, I kept articles and the words "Runner's World" clipped from the magazine's cover. *Runner's World* had been one of my "bibles," the publication that had made me an athlete. So imagine the deep-felt sense of honor I felt when the magazine gave me a Heroes of Running Award in 2005. My acceptance speech appears at the end of this chapter.

How about you? What do you dream about? If you had no restrictions, what would you visualize for your life?

YOUR TURN:

Visualize what you want, now!

———————

*Start putting reminders of what it is you want to become and achieve every-
where. You want to see it and be reminded of it constantly. Let your mind
soak it up like a sponge absorbs water.*

*Today, pick one word that brings you strength and determination, leads
you on a path and energizes you toward taking action on your dreams and
goals. Write the word down on seven different pieces of paper or on things you
carry with you. Place them around your house, tape one onto the fridge, on
your coffee table, place one in your sock drawer, or carry one in your wallet.
Put them in places where you will see the word throughout the day and
be reminded.*

*Create your own Dream Drawer right now. Cut out pictures, sayings,
anything that reminds you of your goals and dreams. Use magazines, photo
albums, ticket stubs, programs, souvenirs-anything! Make a work of art for
your life and fill it up proudly.*

SEVEN THINGS I AM GOING TO PUT
IN MY DREAM DRAWER:

1.

2.

3.

4.

5.

6.

7.

RUNNER'S WORLD MAGAZINE

Heroes of Running Award Acceptance Speech

Life is good, being alive is a gift, and being able to run is just a pure miracle.

Besides the birth of my son, I have never been prouder than to be standing here tonight. To be honored among such incredible athletes-especially my sprinters, who I watch with pride and awe at their thoroughbred beauty in flight. I am so humbled to see myself between the pages of a magazine that for many years while struggling to survive was my inspiration, my dream, my hope.

Ripped-out pages were hung up all over the house for the times I felt like I just couldn't struggle for breath anymore. Hoping that a quick glance at a Nike ad or the picture of a runner "dancing their feet" into the sunset would spark another push in me. Those pictures, this magazine, got me through the tough days…and there were many.

I wanted, I yearned, so bad to run my entire life. To me, other than hearing my son say "momma," there is nothing more beautiful than seeing a "runner in flight," celebrating life and the incredible honor it is to have it. I am a dreamer, and I always will be-I have to be.

I'd like to share with you how I felt the first time I ever got to run 10 years ago at age 28. I got my lung transplant October 1994 and ran in May 1995.

I can still remember lacing up my Nikes knowing that this time; I was really going to use them!

My heart was beating so fast and my lungs…they were working perfectly. Breaths…in and…out.

I was scared but so excited, so ready for this moment. I started.

I couldn't believe it as I saw the grass, then cement, pass under my feet and that I was indeed moving-passing by things. I was now just like the people I watched out the car window or on TV for so many years with such admiration but also heartbreak.

"I was really running!" I thought to myself, and it was the most beautiful and amazing feeling in the world.

I will never forget that birth, that day in May of 1995. Every time I run, to this very day, I feel the joy of a baby taking its first steps. Running to me is life, living, and a pure celebration.

Thank you to everyone at Runner's World for believing in me. For honoring me as one of your Heroes-you are all indeed mine.

I thank you for the kids with cystic fibrosis, for the 20-year-old I just met two days ago who has been waiting for her own lung transplant for three years now, who struggled to breathe as she asked me to sign her own issue so she could go back and hang it up in her hospital room for inspiration.

For the parents who can show their kids "Yes, you can be and do anything you want, even with CF if you fight and hold onto your dreams."

I will never forget this night or weekend as long as I live and cannot wait to tell my son when he is old enough to understand.

I am a girl who was born with cystic fibrosis that was told she would never grow up, never mind run.

Dreams do come true-even ones you would never imagine like tonight. I am so proud to be a runner, and I will be one until the day God calls me home.

Thank you from the bottom of my heart.

Acceptance Speech delivered on November 5, 2005
At the Heroes of Running Awards Ceremony, New York City

A·T·H·**L**·E·T·E

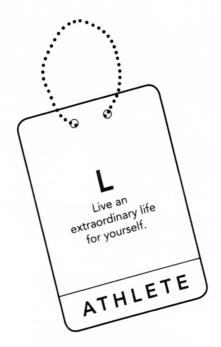

L

Live an
extraordinary life
for yourself.

ATHLETE

Principle 4.

Live your life fully each moment. Living your unique purpose prevents you from becoming one of society's statistics.

"Some days are going to be hard. Nothing worth having ever comes easy but, just when you feel like you're beat and can't stand it anymore, think of someone whose shoes you wouldn't want to walk in. There is always someone whose burden seems like a load you wouldn't be capable of carrying and so you know that yours isn't too much for you and press on knowing that there is purpose in your pain."

-Lauryn Williams, Sub-11 second 100m sprinter,
World Champion/Olympic Medalist

Having someone apply a statistic to my life or use it to predict my chances only motivates me to prove it wrong. How can I be defined by something that hasn't happened yet? Never allow yourself to be counted out or summed up by statistics.

If we rely solely on statistics to weigh our options or measure risks, we give power to the possibility that we might not achieve what we have set out to do.

To stay true to ourselves, we must put everyone else's options and statistics out of our head.

AFFIRMATION:

I Love Myself and My Fierce Determination.

L

LIVE AN EXTRAORDINARY LIFE FOR YOURSELF.

Your life can be ordinary, or your life can be extraordinary. The choice is yours and yours alone. You are presented with many options in life. An option is a choice. Some choices are easy; some are hard.

For a person with a medical condition, options are always tied to a discussion about risks and probable outcomes based on statistics collected from other patients. Remember, other people are not living in your body.

> *"The decisions you make and the actions you take directly determine whether your life will be ordinary or extraordinary."*

In most situations, the only way to fail is to decide to give up. People who have triumphed over insurmountable odds made a decision to put all options and statistics out of their mind and singularly focus on the task at hand and the victory that lies ahead.

You can do this with any situation you face. Do not give yourself any option but to go forward with what it is you want.

It's hard to acknowledge that when your own problems seem so real and insurmountable, that there is always someone who's worse off than you. But take a step back for a moment and think about what you have to be grateful for. No one's life is perfect, but it's a gift nonetheless. It is how you choose to deal with the circumstances that you face that makes your life, this gift, as great as it can be.

MY CYCLE THROUGH LIFE: BIKING WITH CF FREEDOM

One of the greatest lessons my parents taught me was to recognize that there is always someone out there who is sicker or facing bigger problems. I was always taught to be grateful for what I have. They reminded me of this quite often, especially when I complained about having to go to the doctor or have chest PT instead of playing with friends. Or having to eat a well-balanced meal instead of just a sandwich or fast food. They never put a lot of emotion behind their reminders. They stated it as a fact: I was lucky. I knew it too because of what I had seen being around hospitals so much.

I remember one time when I was six or seven walking through the big front doors at Children's Hospital in Boston. I was there for a three-month check-up with Dr. Khaw.

I knew it would be a long day filled with needle sticks, breathing tests, x-rays, and generally being poked and prodded to see how far my disease had progressed. It wasn't going to be fun.

As I entered the building my eyes were drawn, as they always were, to a merry-go-round that stood in the middle of the large waiting area. Six little red bikes went around in a circle, all connected, going nowhere.

I watched kids ride around in circles, holding on tightly to the handlebars. There were kids with burn bandages around various parts of their bodies, kids with no hair from cancer treatment, kids with missing limbs, paralyzed kids, and terminally ill kids. Yet, there they were thoroughly enjoying the moment. Laughing, smiling, living life fully.

I smiled at the kids while holding tightly to my parent's hands as we walked by. I felt really lucky that even though I was about to undergo a battery of tests I could still go home and ride my bike around the neighborhood, not in circles, but freely and under my own power. Even with broken lungs, I felt lucky.

There is one sure way to feel lucky in life even if you are feeling bad about yourself-feel grateful and realize your life is a gift. Take a walk through the pediatric ward of a hospital. Look at the faces of children tangled up in tubes, bent over from pain, or struggling just to stay alive. You will surely see that your life, no matter how rough, is a gift to be appreciated and cherished.

FORCED TO SIT OUT:
DETERMINED TO MAKE A STAND

In grade school, I had been admitted to the hospital many times for infections. My lungs had certainly declined, but I didn't consider myself sick.

However, I was short of breath, a lot. My CF had shown a lot of asthmatic effects, and my airways were very tight most of the time. Whereas others could cough and get the "junk" out easily, I was tight and dry. It might take me a half hour to get out a little speck. It was extremely challenging to get air into my lungs.

I somehow managed to continue taking gym class and muscled through it by going into the corner of the room to take deep breaths or escaping to the bathroom for coughing fits. The most difficult parts of gym class were activities that required me to be active for long periods of time.

I remember one day in particular. We 7th-graders were going to do the mile run for the physical fitness test. Dressed in our one-piece, blue-and-white Bobcat gym uniforms, we made our way to a parking lot where the run would start. I panicked. The teacher knew I had CF, but none of the kids really understood what it was or how serious it was except for a few close friends.

As my classmates jumped around to keep warm, I was sweating. Not from jumping around, I was sweating from worrying about being singled out and told I couldn't participate. All of my classmate's faces were focused on the teacher as he explained the mile route. I looked at the ground, wanting to disappear.

As the kids started to line up, my gym teacher made a motion toward me as if he were swatting away a fly. He gestured vigorously for me to go and sit on the curb.

For a quick second I just wanted to quit and walk home. He crushed my spirit that day. But just for a moment. I didn't quit. It made me 1,000 times more motivated.

There are things that have happened in my life that I believe were blessings in disguise. Being shooed to the curb was one of the biggest ones. In fact it may have been the defining moment of my life.

I wasn't thinking about giving up back then. Instead, I sat down as instructed and kept my head down so I didn't have to watch my friends and classmates take off and disappear over a hill doing the very thing I dreamed about. I can still feel the rocks and gravel that I played with under my Nikes to keep myself busy.

The humiliation I felt sitting there on the curb was like no sensation I had ever experienced before. No needle insertion, no lung infection, no clean-out, surgery, nothing else compared to the pain and yearning I felt that day as I heard the whistle blow.

I allowed the anger I felt toward my gym teacher and the pain of having to sit out to become fuel for achieving what I wanted most. I vowed that I would never be forced to sit on the sidelines again, ever. I would do whatever it took. I embedded it in my mind, heart, and soul. One day. I would not only run but sprint up that hill. Come hell or high water, I would run the whole mile.

I would be an athlete. I just didn't realize at the time what hell would be or how high the water would become. What I did know was that the next time I would not be sitting on that curb. I would be running as hard and as fast as I could, breathing deep and running free.

WE ARE MARATHONERS: OUR RELAY OF LIFE

In April 1994, six months before I received my working lungs, a group of us from Mass General did something none of us could do alone and something that no one thought we could. We became marathon runners.

The Boston Marathon was coming up. A group of us with CF decided to form a CF relay team and run the Boston Marathon.

At first our doctors thought we were crazy, but the more they saw us plan they realized how excited we were about defying the odds. No doctor who treats CF could ignore that.

We applied as a charity team to the Boston Athletic Association, organizers of the Boston Marathon, but they turned us down. We understood but that didn't stop us. We ran anyway as "unofficial runners."

Our plan to run was headed up by my good friend Mary Dunn. She had run full marathons but was now at the point in her battle with CF where she couldn't run a full one.

She knew what it was like to have limitations and struggle at times for breath. Mary also knew what it felt like to accomplish a dream, which was why she came up with the idea to have a group of us do the marathon. Excited and with a flame ignited within each of us, we took the idea and "ran" with it.

Sixteen of us, along with our doctors and a few nurses, ran our hearts out that day. We passed a baton with a red rose painted on it to signify 65 roses, which sounds like and represents "cystic fibrosis." Mary and I designed the logo, a red rose wrapped around a burning torch, for our t-shirts, which proudly declared MGH CF Marathon Relay Team.

Prior to the race I was scared to death. My section of the relay was 25.5 miles to 26 miles, near the race finish line. My dad and Dr. Lapey, one of our CF doctors, ran the entire half-mile marathon beside me, while I attempted to jog by scraping my feet across the ground.

Buoyed by my desire and the support of my friends and family, fear gave way to joy. It was amazing being surrounded and passed by what we called "real" runners. When I turned the corner onto the famous Boylston Street, I knew one day I would take this turn really running and smiled knowing that I was working toward that goal that very moment.

I then passed the baton to my good friend Shawn who had received his lung transplant only months before. I made for the side of the street and almost passed out as I tried to catch my breath, but I felt too alive to give in to my body's weariness. I picked up a foil blanket discarded by another runner and wrapped it around me like a medal.

I was exhausted when we returned to the hospital after the race. Because I was still undergoing a clean-out, I had run the race with a covered-up IV port in my arm.

We had a little party at the hotel across from the hospital and gave Dr. Khaw the rose baton we had all clasped during our half-mile. We were all smiling, laughing, coughing, and living. Really living.

We were in pure celebration of life. Together we did what none of us could do alone. No one could tell us that day, or any other, that we weren't all marathon runners.

It's OK to ask others for help. Never be afraid to reach out. There is great strength in numbers and sometimes that's what you need to get you further down your path. Sometimes it takes courage to realize what you cannot do alone.

MY OLYMPIC TORCH RUN: LUNG TRANSPLANT SPRINTER

Just when I thought maybe I could "retire" for a bit from running and hide until I got better, I received a letter in the mail. I had been nominated by my sister to carry the Olympic torch in the Chevrolet Olympic Torch Relay for the 2002 Winter Olympics.

I should've been elated and proud, but I was scared to death. How was I going to do this when I had trouble walking up the three steps to my house?

The day of the event was on my 36th birthday, December 27, 2001. According to the letter the torch I was to carry would be made out of lightweight titanium. The run itself was only two-tenths of a mile, a marathon to me at this point. What's more, HBO Real Sports wanted to film it. No pressure, no pressure at all! Just the potential to fail on national television.

This should have been easy, but I had 20 pounds of fluid retention in my body and failing kidneys. I was on dialysis. Should I even try? "Don't try," I told myself, "Just do it."

I didn't have to accept this honor. Believe me, I thought about saying "no thank you" many times as I read the letter over and over with shaking hands and weak legs. I wondered how I was going to run two-tenths of a mile while carrying a torch. I had to figure out how.

I knew deep inside that I couldn't afford to say no. It would be like accepting defeat, allowing myself to give up. Any sign of giving up at this point when I was so sick would mean I was done for. My spirit and my life would die out.

I also knew I had to do it for my family. They were in agony watching me get sicker and sicker. They knew I was hanging on by threads to make it through each day. I had to prove to them, to everyone who knew and cared for me, to myself, and especially to every little kid I had encouraged to keep going that I wasn't a quitter. Now, more than ever, was the time to practice what I preached.

The morning of the relay still sticks with me. I puked and had to have help getting dressed into my official Olympic white-and-baby blue relay uniform. I made sure I wore matching white Nikes. I placed the official hat with Olympic rings over my hair, which was half as thick as it once was. I was now properly suited up for the mission.

Once in Boston, I was put in a room with all the other chosen ones. We waited for a van to pick us up and drop us off at our marked places along the course. As I looked around at the other runners, all of whom seemed a lot stronger and way more prepared than me, I thought, "Oh my God, Dottie, you had better do this. Just make it through and carry this thing and you can go home and sleep." I was concerned about dropping the torch if it got too heavy, but I was more worried about not being able to run with it.

I had to take control of my fear, because I knew if I gave into it my body would too, and it would all be over. "Maybe if I jog really, really slow I can drag my legs the two-tenths of a mile," I tried to convince myself. "Maybe I'll be carried along by the excitement of the crowd along the route," I thought. I had heard marathoners say that, and I hoped that my short route would be lined with "screamers."

"Please let my determination and desire to fight carry me through," I prayed. Just as I was taking a deep breath in prayer I heard my name being called. The van was ready for me. Here we go body, let's do this.

Once in the van, I was introduced to the person who would be running with me. He knew my story and would go as slowly as I wanted. He smiled and patted me assuredly on the back. "I'm glad someone's confident," I thought as I looked up at him, smiled, and said "OK."

Without giving me any time to back out, the van quickly stopped, and I was told to jump out and was handed my torch. The runner before me stopped and lit mine.

I struggled to hold up the Olympic torch. I felt an immediate sense of pride and excitement as I started to run. Within seconds, I realized I had nothing. My legs just didn't want to move. My heart was pumping, my lungs were breathing in and out, but my legs felt like cement. Every part of me wanted to go fast except my legs.

I looked at my runner and said, "I think I'm going to walk a little," and I slowed down. I hated saying those words, but the torch felt heavy as I fought to hold it up high and struggled even harder to smile at the crowd. I was proud but dying inside, my spirit was being broken. But I realized where I was at this point in my life and felt grateful that I was even walking.

I thanked God for the pain I was feeling. Pain reminds me that I'm alive, and I fought hard to remember that as I hurt in my legs and in my heart. Through my discomfort, I remembered how lucky I was to be alive and walked proudly past the people who were cheering exuberantly for me.

When I heard one of the officials yell that I would soon be passing the Olympic torch to another runner, I gave it all I had. The Dottie that slammed into that old rusty fence had to come out right now!

She did. I started to run again, I made my leaden legs fight and lift off the ground. Step by step I slowly jogged toward the next runner. Once I was close enough, I stopped and reached forward with my beautiful torch to light the one waiting.

I did it! I was so tired when I finished and so glad it was over. I was also so proud of myself because I truly did not know if I could accomplish this amazing feat.

Put on your battle gear and live an extraordinary life.
Sometimes I paint my toenails black for "battle" or write
"Be Fearless" with a marker on the inside of my wrist. It might
sound silly, but it works for me. Do your own thing. Customizing
a motivational tool for yourself will help you stay focused.
Do not allow yourself to give in. Yes, you can allow yourself
to have a bad day or a day of rest but if it gets to be a couple
days, make sure on the third day you get up and get over it.
If that sounds harsh, well, it's only because I believe you
can do it! If I can, so can you. Sometimes it helps to be
accountable to someone else, so find a buddy or simply know
that I too am "getting over it" on my third day,
Never, ever give up! You can do it!

YOUR TURN:

Choose to live an extraordinary life!

Think of seven things that have been constant limiting factors in your life. These are your obstacles. These seven roadblocks make you question yourself and get in the way of your dreams. Don't surrender to them, face them head on, and take responsibility for them. Embrace those fears or doubts then make them go away. Find ways to chip away at them like jewelers chip away at a diamond to create brilliant facets.

If your obstacle is self-doubt, tell yourself you can do it or reach out to someone who will remind you that you can. If your obstacle is lack of understanding, become educated because knowledge is power. Whatever your obstacles are, write them down. Next to each obstacle, write a course of action that will allow you to overcome it.

Extraordinary choices will make your dreams come true. Make up your own affirmations, make a choice to say "I will, I can, and I am."

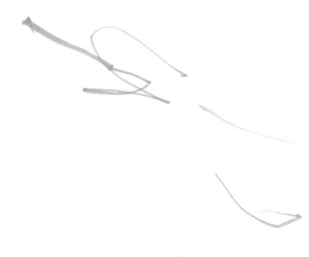

SEVEN OBSTACLES THAT PREVENT ME FROM LEADING AN EXTRAORDINARY LIFE:

1.

2.

3.

4.

5.

6.

7.

SEVEN ACTION STEPS THAT ALLOW ME
TO OVERCOME MY OBSTACLES:

1.

2.

3.

4.

5.

6.

7.

A·T·H·L·E·T·E

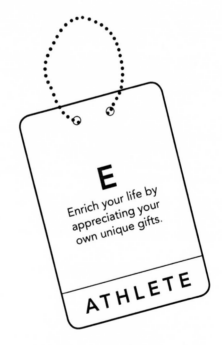

Principle 5.

Enjoy every single moment of your life. Be especially grateful for it and everything that enriches it.

"To give anything less than your best is to sacrifice the Gift."

-Steve Prefontaine, 1972 U.S. Olympic runner

Appreciation of life is a gift you must give yourself daily. The next time you step out into the world take notice of all the joyful things life has to offer: a child's laughter, the smell of a flower, or the playfulness of a puppy. Make a conscious effort each day to see the world in color instead of black and white. Practice making gratitude lists, especially on the days you feel your life isn't so great.

We can all make simple decisions to enjoy life and the world around us. We have a choice how to live and what we will focus on. Being grateful for life and truly appreciating this gift allows you to keep difficult events and situations in perspective. It gives you a foundation to remain positive in even the most challenging of circumstances. You will receive many gifts in life when you live it with appreciation.

AFFIRMATION:

I Am Extremely Grateful for My Life.

E

ENRICH YOUR LIFE BY APPRECIATING YOUR OWN UNIQUE GIFTS.

We all are born into this life with a unique set of gifts: being able to play music, making breakthroughs in medicine or science, inspiring others in a classroom, being a nurturing parent, changing policies through activism, or competing as an athlete. Whatever your gifts are, you need to recognize, understand, and appreciate them. They are unique to you. Do whatever you can to enrich your set of gifts.

Open up whatever is in your own boxes and enjoy the unique gifts inside. If you don't celebrate the unique gifts you have, then you aren't living.

"Although I would never wish living with a "terminal" disease on anyone, I do wish people could be blessed by the perspective on life that I have because I live with a terminal disease. Every day is truly gift. I am uniquely aware of and eternally grateful for every breath I take. I believe with every trial comes great opportunities for learning and growth and I can honestly thank my disease for teaching me this invaluable lesson."

-Sharlie Ross Kaltenbach

SURE OF MYSELF: NOT ALLOWING MYSELF TO BE A STATISTIC

I want you to consider a question that people ask me all the time, "What causes you to keep going?" "I didn't have an option," I respond. "Well, of course you did," they argue.

Do they really think there was or is an option? All I have known how to do is to fight for my life and the things I wanted. I wouldn't know how to give up if I wanted to. How do I make my heart stop? Do I hold my breath until I turn blue and pass out, do I stop taking my meds?

Is there any other option but to live for as long and as strong and happy as I can until I go out, fighting? I was not made to give up. I don't think anyone is. My whole life I was expected to be a statistic, and I hated it. I am not a statistic, nor will I ever be and neither should you.

If I followed what statistics said I would not have been around to write this book, and my parents would not have seen me through first grade.

*"Being called a statistic motivates me to succeed.
Don't include me in something that hasn't happened yet."*

Never allow yourself to be counted out. Only you can be the one to decide that. You decide right now.

"Conquer it before it conquers you."
My gift to you from Donna "Momma" Williams.

Respect doctors, knowledge, science, and mentors. However, respect yourself more. Your soul knows what is best for you. Respect your beliefs, dreams, and goals more. A lot more. Do not allow others' negative thoughts get inside you. Let them bounce off your chest like a ball.

I remember the way people would look at me after my mother told them I had CF. Some had pity in their eyes as if they were looking at a hungry, homeless animal. I didn't want anyone to feel that way for me. I just wanted to be normal and not have people look at me differently.

I returned their stares with my eyes intensely burning as if to say, "That's not me," and I quickly turned to go play. Other times I would just smile or try to look right through them.

Whatever I did, I made sure that my thoughts immediately went into action-what could I do at that moment to show them I wasn't someone to pity? I would pop out my chest and stand tall or go and play, move.

I guess in some ways I was in their face. I hadn't meant to be rude, but I wanted to let them know that I had a goal-to be healthy and alive, an athlete, to be able to run, compete in whatever sport I wanted. I wasn't going to give up, and I'd show them by doing the things they didn't think I could do.

When I was admitted to the hospital for lung clean-outs, which usually lasted between 10 and 14 days, I wouldn't only pack my clothes, toothbrush, and toothpaste. I would arrive with a huge gym bag filled with ammunition.

I brought a blender and protein powder, five-and ten-pound dumbbells, a good workout video, some motivational books, and pictures ripped out from Runner's World and fitness magazines.

Proper nutrition and regular exercise enriches your life.

Once in my room, no matter how badly I felt, I took out the clippings of pictures and sayings and taped them over the hospital pictures that hung on the walls. I covered up anything I could that was medical and made it hopeful. I always put the "Just Do It" sign under the clock to remind me it was "time" to move. I let the rest sit in the bag for the first couple of days until I could feel the meds starting to fight the infection. Then I began to "unwrap."

I pulled out my dumbbells and placed them on the shelf next to a box of tissues. I placed my blender next to the dumbbells and put my motivational books near the container that held used needles. I was ready to begin.

Sometimes I was lucky enough to get a private room, but there were many times I had a roommate. There was no floor reserved for young adults with CF, so we were mixed in with the general population. I often found myself sharing a room with a sweet elderly woman. My older roommates reminded me that if I lived my purpose, I could live a long life as well.

I still chuckle when I think about the time after a very heartfelt discussion with one of my elderly roommates about being aware and living every second of life in the present moment, she got up and mistook my suitcase for a toilet.

I was friendly with my roommates, but I usually kept my curtain pulled. Not too many patients were accustomed to having a mini-gym right next to them. I almost gave one of my roomies a heart attack one night when I turned on the blender to make a post-workout protein shake. After that the head nurse told my parents they had to take my blender home. However, the floor nurses rallied for me to keep my blender in their break room. They rocked!

It was sort of funny to see how surprised my roommates' visitors were when they poked their heads past the curtain to say hello and saw my set-up. Who knows what they expected to see having heard the sounds of a blender, loud coughing, and vomiting coming from my side, sometimes all at once.

It was my sanctuary, though. It had to be. There were nights when I would lie in bed totally afraid, listening to the beeping of my heart monitor and tied to an IV and oxygen. I would hear the calls of pain from patients down the hall or sometimes right next to me. I would stare at a picture of a runner striding across a road or the picture of a muscular body standing proudly. The reminder to "just do it" kept me grounded to where I needed to be-getting better, healing to be one day closer to my goal of being healthy.

I couldn't allow myself to give up, to give in to the situations I was
dealt. So many times I would have welcomed staying in bed all day
with the covers over my head but no way. If I did that, then my body
would know I was willing to stop moving. I never allowed my body to
stop moving, to allow my disease to win. I had to fight it every way I
could. I didn't give up, and therefore my body didn't either. I would
not become a statistic, anyone's statistic.

UNDERSTANDING MY GIFTS:
DYING TWICE ON THE OPERATING TABLE

Waiting for the sedative to kick in under the bright lights of
the operating room, I smiled. I knew I had prepared my body
as best as I could have for the battle to come. I had made my
peace with God and my transplant surgeon Dr. Wain. I had
been worried how he might feel if I didn't make it. I had told
him with great belief that whatever happened I would be OK,
because either way I would soon be able to breathe. Either
here on earth or in Heaven.

Dr. Wain needed to know once again that he was my
hero. I saw his cheeks wrinkle around the blue surgical mask
as I held his soft hand in mine. I smiled as I fell asleep with the
thought of waking up running.

But my lungs were really tired. No one knew how much
my lungs had deteriorated until they opened me up on the

table. Inside this body of self-made armor were lungs that were failing fast and should've given out a long, long time ago. The surgery was very difficult.

My lungs had to be literally scraped out of my body piece by piece. It took 12 hours to remove the mess that CF had reduced my lungs to: eight hours for the right lung and four hours for the left.

My heart stopped twice during the surgery. I had actually died two times. I remember drifting between here and a wonderful place that seemed like Heaven.

I had to be put on a heart/lung machine, and they almost lost me for good. Somehow I made it through. My post-operative condition was so serious, I had to be given drugs to put me in an induced coma.

The doctors had wanted to keep me in that state for a few days to give me extra time to heal from this extraordinarily difficult surgery. But they reluctantly decided to revive me, because I was fighting too hard to wake up on my own.

When I was conscious and able to speak, I thanked Dr. Wain for saving my life. "Don't thank me, Dottie," he said, "If you hadn't been in the great shape you were in, you wouldn't be here. Just keep doing what you're doing," he smiled.

I thanked God for giving me the strength to not quit or let go. I now comprehended fully how life, all of it, was indeed a gift. And now that I understood how valuable this gift was, I was determined more than ever not to give it up.

Now that I had healthy lungs living inside of me, I redirected my focus and changed the direction of my purpose. I had to do everything I could to protect what was underneath my chest-lungs that could breathe and allow me to run.

After almost a month of recovery in the hospital, the infectious disease doctors sat me down and told me everything I couldn't do, everything I had to watch out for being immune suppressed, everything that could happen "if." They were only doing their jobs, but during that 15-minute visit they scared the hell out of me. "Don't take these new lungs away please, please...," I prayed.

I was afraid of everything, anyone who coughed, tried to shake my hand, or attempted to give me a hug. I was petrified of those big ugly germs. I was terrified of anything that could make me sick and wreak havoc in my life. I had gone through so much to get my lungs and now, in a moment, if I weren't careful, they could be gone.

So again, I suited up for battle. It had been suggested that in the first few months of recovery I take extra precautions. The doctors told me to wear a mask in crowded places, in the hospital, around anyone who was sick, the list went on. That's all I needed to hear. I wore a mask everywhere but that didn't seem to be enough. What if a germ got through? So, I wore three masks, one on top of the other. There was no way anything was going to make me sick and jeopardize the new healthy lungs that I had waited all my life for.

This was my gift after all. However, I was reminded a couple months after my transplant by someone pretty special that gifts are meant to be unwrapped, opened, celebrated, and used.

You make the choice. You can either choose to walk with your head held high, allowing yourself to see the sky and feel the sun on your face, or you can choose to walk with your head hung low, seeing nothing but the ground underneath you. It is your attitude and the way you look at your life that determines how it will be lived. Appreciate the little things and look to find the good in all situations. There is freedom in being able to take a deep breath, being able to laugh, being able to reach out and touch another life. Live your life fully and richly.

Dr. Wain had asked me to speak with him in front of a group of residents. I was honored and, yes, I wore my mask, two in fact. We spoke a little before the conference, and he told me how thrilled he was that I was healing so well and making plans to live my life. Although he didn't say anything, I know he saw the two elastic bands wrapped around my head. With a silent understanding that didn't make me feel stupid or silly, he gave me a really good piece of advice that I have never forgotten and share with whomever I can.

"Dottie, you know how when you get a new pair of sneakers you don't just keep them in the box?" he asked. I nodded. "You take them out and wear them. You especially would run with them, right? That's what I want you to do with your new lungs. I want you to take them out, unwrap them, use them, and live and run with them. Be cautious but do everything you have waited to do."

I finally got it. As I looked at this incredible man, who I believe was put on this earth in part to save my life, I realized that he had given me another gift. He gave me permission to live life fully, to let my lungs free like butterfly wings.

I began to embrace my gifts. I started to take the mask off. I would go into stores that weren't crowded without a mask on, then see friends, hug them, kiss them on the cheek. With every fear that didn't come true, little by little I began to untie ribbons from the gifts I had been given. Soon, like a new pair of sneakers, I took my new lungs right out of the box and ran with them, fearlessly celebrating my gift of life. Be fearless as much as you can because it allows you to live life in an extraordinary way.

THE GIFT OF LIFE:
LIVING BY THE GRACE OF OTHERS

I am so grateful for my life. I may have been born with a disease that caused me to struggle, but it also allowed me to see the world in color instead of black and white. I feel so blessed that there are people who make the choice to be an organ donor. How can you ever be grateful enough to someone who saves your life? You live the best life you can to honor what has been given to you.

Look at the front cover of this book. Do you see the number 1027 on the athlete tag? That number is the month and day (10-27) in 1994 I received my new lungs. It's a day I will never forget. A day when I died and was born again, rising from the ashes of my old body with new pink lungs, able to breathe fully and deeply for the first time.

It's also a time of mixed emotions. It marks the anniversary of the death of the man who gave me my transplant gift. I am always filled with such appreciation, yet there is sadness in my heart for a courageous family that chose to give the gift of life. They mourn when I celebrate.

On the second-year anniversary, I decided to share the day with "him," my lung donor. I didn't want to visit his grave or mourn, so I figured out a way to pay tribute to his life.

I knew exactly the perfect way to do just that-by climbing a mountain. You see as God would have it, my donor was a mountain climber, an athlete! I drove to a small mountain in New Hampshire, where I left a yellow rose wrapped in a green ribbon to commemorate our climb together. It really felt as if his spirit were with me that day.

Since the transplant, I have felt at home in the mountains. Is it cellular memory or is it because Dr. Khaw told me I received a mountain climber's lungs? I don't know. I just know I feel a certain peace within when I look at a beautiful picture of mountains, drive through them, or even fly over them.

Each year on October 27, "we" climb mountains, and my breaths are deep for him. I pay special attention to the steps I take as I climb upward. I pause and wonder, did he step on these exact same rocks? I smile with pride knowing I am bringing him back to what he loved to do. I make sure to take in everything-the sweet sound of my breaths, dew on the leaves, strong roots in the earth, and the sunlight that always seems to shine through the trees like a moonbeam at just the right clearing-to remind me that I am not alone and we are living life together.

If you were to see me climbing, you would see me smile and you'd see a few tears, too. When I get to the top of the mountain or a place where I feel God is smiling down upon me, I pull the yellow rose out from my backpack and kneel down. I say "thank you" and place the rose down upon the mountain as a memory of a life lived and then passed on.

From a state of grace and gratitude, live your life in an extraordinary manner by never forgetting to acknowledge whatever enriches your life.

YOUR TURN:

What enriches your life?

Make a list today and write down everything you can think of that you feel enriches your life. Even the things you may think are silly or too simple are important to add. Keep this list rolled up and tied with ribbon or a shoelace and open it up, as if it were a treasure map to your life, on days when you feel you may need some extra help to find your way. For the next seven days, write down at least seven things that have enriched your life each day.

SEVEN THINGS THAT ENRICH MY LIFE:

1.

2.

3.

4.

5.

6.

7.

A·T·H·L·E·T·E

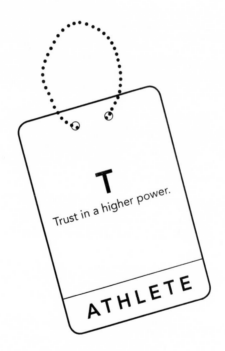

Principle 6.

Tend to your own spiritual foundation on a regular basis.

"When you have love and faith in your life you can overcome almost anything. I live my life and have taught my girls to believe that no matter how difficult the challenges, never give up, be in control of your own destiny, believe in yourself and try to be positive. Life is often difficult but through adversity comes empowerment. I believe that we are where we are supposed to be and that everything in life happens for a reason."

-Vanessa Underwood, motivational speaker, fitness expert, mentor, two-time kidney transplant recipient, cancer survivor

If we live life in the absence of spirituality, we don't have anything to lean on but ourselves and others when times are tough. Often we require something greater, something stronger, something more powerful. Letting go and having faith go hand in hand. The harder we cling to fears or resist things, the more they seem to appear in our life.

AFFIRMATION:

Today Is Another Opportunity to Trust in a Loving Higher Power.

T

TRUST IN A HIGHER POWER.

There is a power greater than us. It's the force that provides structure and meaning to the universe. Being grateful for what you have connects you to this higher, loving power. Living your purpose fully connects you to this force.

Faith in this higher power, in whatever form it takes, provides you with a solid foundation when it feels like you are all alone. It is the cutoff point for emptiness.

If you were falling off a cliff, it is the branch sticking out just far enough for you to grab. It is the bright light that seems to surround you when you feel at peace within yourself.

The more we have faith and trust in God, our higher power, or whatever you call it, the more we can begin to let go of resistance and open ourselves to attracting the results we are looking for on our journey.

I believe everyone needs something to believe in, whether you call it
God or a higher power, some sort of spiritual foundation.
Whatever it is for you, just find it and believe in it. If I didn't have
my faith in God and in Heaven I would never have been able
to handle the things I have had to deal with.

"Believe that you are not alone, ever, and if you want to talk
or pray, someone or something is always listening."

TRUSTING AND SEEING FROM WITHIN: GOD CREATES THE COLORS

It was a prerequisite that anyone having a lung transplant undergo sinus surgery first. Bacteria that could infect the lungs had to be removed from the sinuses. The doctors wanted to get the sinus cavities as clean as they could prior to transplant, hoping nothing infectious would drop into the new lungs.

I wasn't looking forward to having my face cut up, but I knew that if I wanted my lungs I had to do it. It was so bad that my own dad didn't even recognize me when I was wheeled back into the hospital room. My mother had to convince him I was his daughter "Dottie Ann."

My face was so swollen I couldn't hardly see through the slits that were once my eyes. I spent four days nearly blind. Thankfully my ears still worked. I was able to hear the nurses yell for me to breathe through my mouth whenever my oxygen levels began to drop as a result of breathing through my nose.

Not being able to see was even more difficult at night when I was tired. I felt so alone that I would listen for footsteps in the hallway just to know I wasn't. I wanted to know why this was necessary. Through prayer I got my answer: I wanted to live.

Although I had to do some real soul searching I realized that the effects of sinus surgery were actually a blessing. I had made it through the operation even though the doctors had been concerned about my lungs holding up under anesthesia. I found out later that Dr. Khaw had been in the operating room during surgery, not to assist but to "make the call" if I had died.

The second night after surgery when I was finally off the machines, I decided to wander down to the chapel. It was about 2 a.m., and I left a note for Lil, the night nurse, that read, "Went down to chapel, I'm fine, I'll be right back." With that, I let my faith, rather than my blurry and severely limited vision, lead me.

I slid the palm of my hand along the wooden railing using it as my guide. My fingers traced the numbers on the elevator buttons until I found the number one. I rode the elevator down to the first floor. As I walked into the chapel, I could feel the stained glass windows. Although I couldn't really see them, the colors engulfed me.

I knelt down to pray and stayed there for about an hour. Through my blurred vision I saw others come in to write in the prayer book or light a candle. A sense of deep peace grew within me as I felt their worries lift through prayer. They did not walk out the same way they walked in.

I thought, "See Dottie, prayer works, and God always does listen." As I wiped away the first post-surgical tear to fall down my cheek, I smiled from eye slit to eye slit. I thanked God once again for my life and the hope I would continue to have about my future. I returned to my room feeling stronger.

MY HEART STOPPED TWICE:
I WAS PUSHED BACK FROM HEAVEN

I don't really talk about dying much because I choose to focus on living. But I think it's important to talk about it here, because being so close to death taught me how to fight for my own life and for others, too.

Although they were often frustrated with my stubborn-ness, my doctors also admired it. I wanted to live and I wanted to start ASAP. Do the transplant immediately. Start today. That was my mantra.

Even unconscious in the post-operative induced coma, I wouldn't let go. New lungs were inside me, even though they were too big and had to be cut to fit. Even though my chest was bleeding all over the place through wrapped bandages, I wanted to use my new lungs now. I wanted to be awake so badly that it was stressing my body more to be under than it would be to cut short the coma intended to help my body heal, adjust, and rebuild.

Once awake, I had to communicate through notes because I couldn't talk with the ventilator that was helping me breathe. The first note was to my parents telling them I was "OK" and that I loved them. The second note read, "They pushed me back." My family was perplexed.

Once I could talk, I explained to them what I had meant in that cryptic note. When my heart had stopped during surgery, I had experienced my two friends Joey and Penny, who had died from CF, telling me that it was not my time to die. I had also sensed the distinct scent of my Grampie, who died when I was 12.

When I found out that my heart had stopped twice during the surgery, I knew then that I had visited Heaven. My family told me that while I was in the induced coma I kept pointing toward the ceiling and moving my head as if I were trying to talk. They thought I was hallucinating.

I have always believed in God and in Heaven. I have had too many people taken away from me too soon not to.

Joey, who I call "courage in a little package," was like a little brother to me and the first friend I lost to CF. We met in the hospital when I was 16 and he was 10. Over the next two years he taught me about life, laughter, and, most importantly, courage. Joey was tiny in size but giant in spirit. I learned so much from him. When he died, it was enough to remind me daily that I had to be brave and walk with my head held high to fight this disease, not only for me now but for him, too.

Penny was my best friend with CF. We met when we

were 11. Dr. Khaw put us together for a reason, he had a plan. He knew my CF was progressing and that I really didn't have a clue what it all meant, so he figured he would show me firsthand. Penny was pretty sick already and had been in and out of the hospital several times. He admitted us to the hospital as roommates so that together we could be part of a month-long research study at MIT. I thought she knew it all, and she thought I was a spoiled brat. We were both right.

We became like sisters after that, and my parents loved her like a daughter. For 10 years she taught me courage and how to fight this disease with grace and strength.

One conversation we had will forever stay etched in my heart. She made me promise that if she were to die I would be OK and that I would fight and live for "us." We had made a pact that if one of us died the other would continue to fight for life. I never wanted to promise her that because I was afraid that she would use that as a green light to leave.

Despite my fear, I gave her my promise because she was my best friend and she deserved that from me. I knew what she was asking me, and I knew she needed to hear my response. The moment I did I heard her emit the biggest sigh of air I had ever heard come from her—clear and without struggle. It was beautiful, and I knew what I had just done. Once I hung up the phone, I collapsed on the bathroom floor in a heap of broken dreams, crying. I sat there and prayed to God to help me get up and face the world, now for the two of us.

Three short days later, I prayed again while holding Penny's hand as she finally let go and went to Heaven. When

I saw peace come over her withered body as her tired lungs finally rested, it was one of the most beautiful experiences of my life.

My grandfather, my dad's dad, was probably the greatest man beside my father I have ever known. He always wore the same olive-green, button-down sweater, and he had his own "Grampie" smell. He made me sing "Hot Cross Buns" whenever we were driving in the car together. He taught me about looking extra hard at the beauty of life. No matter how bad it seemed.

When my heart stopped during surgery, Joey, Penny, and my Grampie all made their presence known. I was at the tip of Heaven and knew God was all around me because he brought to me the people I loved when I needed them most. While I didn't actually see my grandfather, the smell of his sweater was as strong as a freshly baked apple pie put right under my nose. He was there by my side.

As for Penny and Joey, they looked different. Penny didn't have her trademark tan, and Joey didn't have his starry blue eyes. They were just there in my presence like transparent shadows, shadows of brilliant luminous light, with an unconditional loving energy.

I was going through a tunnel or hallway. I was enveloped with a bright loving light and I experienced a calmness I had never known. Wherever I was, I wanted to stay, but Joey and Penny were adamant that I had to return.

These souls were my angels who were with God and pushed me back. I knew I had been saved. I knew it from the moment my eyes opened and was awakened to sounds of beeping and ringing in the intensive care unit. God wasn't ready for me yet, and my friends needed me to continue to fight to prove that CF doesn't always win.

I told anyone who would listen for days after the ventilator was removed that Joey and Penny had pushed me back and that I had smelled my Grampie. I also remember the deep need to call Joey's parents, Joe and Kathy O'Donnell, and to tell them Joey was OK.

Joey was healthy and happy. I knew this for a fact now. His lungs were perfect. He could run, jump, and play without being out of breath.

I had a new peace about myself that things would be OK, and I felt a new sense of determination to keep fighting so that I might be an inspiration to others. I continue to call upon that moment during difficult situations, and I thank God for saving my life and for giving me heroes to remind me why my fight is necessary.

I miss all of the friends that I have lost to CF, daily. There are too many to count, but I take a piece of them with me in all I do.

During competitions, I often write their names on my arms so that they are with me in spirit, running, climbing over walls, and sprinting with me. Penny and Joey are always at the top of the list.

I am not perfect, not even close. I have made mistakes and some bad decisions, but I believe that everything happens for a reason. I try to show how thankful I am for my life, all of it, by talking to God throughout the day, through every struggle and every joy. Never forgetting there is someone with larger problems praying also.

Prayer really has worked for me, because I believe my higher power is always listening and I know it requires me to listen, too. My friend Ryan Hall best summed it up this way.

"I am able to push myself harder, faster, and normally outside of my physical limitations when I am focused on Him and not on my pain, competitors, or split times. One of the things I am most certain of, based on my experiences of living both God's way and my way, is that His way is better than my way and that the closer I am following Him the more I enjoy life. If there is only one thing I can pass on to others it is this."

-Ryan Hall, elite marathon runner, 2008 Olympian

YOUR TURN:

How do you communicate with your higher power?

One way is to simply say "thank you" throughout the day. Words of gratitude are words of power that bring you joy. Just be grateful. Miracles happen from a state of gratitude.

Prayer works, try it if you haven't yet. Just start a conversation with God or your higher power. Find some sort of spirituality that fits you. Use it as your foundation. Just pray silently. Find a way to do it that suits you and is comfortable. I have prayed and had conversations in the strangest places. I guarantee you it will be worth it.

On the next page, write down your own prayers and seven things you are grateful for. Use this page as a launching pad for your own miracles.

MY PRAYER TO MY HIGHER POWER.

SEVEN THINGS I AM THANKFUL FOR:

1.

2.

3.

4.

5.

6.

7.

A·T·H·L·E·T·E

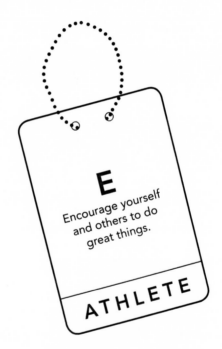

E

Encourage yourself
and others to do
great things.

ATHLETE

Principle 7.

Each day is a new opportunity to raise the bar.

---

*"Never limit where running (life) can take you because each race (day)
has the potential for adventure (living)."*

-Bart Yasso, chief running officer, Runner's World magazine,
and author of My Life on the Run

When it comes to living your purpose you must be willing to reach higher. Think about your next goal, so you can continue to climb forward steadfastly and with determination. Decide what you want, then focus on it. Believe you can have it, and take it.

Allow that flicker to accept the wind and turn into a flame that burns with another desire, another life goal. Be grateful for your achievements but never stop reaching, raising the bar.

AFFIRMATION:

Excellence is Always within My Reach Today.

E

ENCOURAGE YOURSELF AND OTHERS TO DO GREAT THINGS.

A life lived with purpose is always in motion. When we are in motion and taking action, goals can be achieved at a faster rate than we ever perceived. We must not be afraid to want more and succeed beyond the goals what we have set for ourselves. Oftentimes, we can be our own limitation.

> *"When success arrives don't be surprised.*
> *Enjoy, savor and embrace every second of it."*

Sometimes when people achieve what they have been dreaming about, they act bewildered, as if they really hadn't expected it. They promptly go to work dismantling their successes or thinking of them as the single crowning moments of their lives, never to be reached again.

When you achieve success, take some time to direct your attention to your next great achievement. Renew and reset your passion, focus, and your energy towards it.

Do not let new fears or the unknown stop you in your

tracks. Force yourself to demand more and set higher bars, you will be more fulfilled. Set new goals daily to achieve greater things. Having goals is like wearing a life preserver, they keep you afloat.

"Mastery over doubt-nothing paramount has ever been achieved except by those who dared to believe in something inside them was superior to circumstance."

-Nike

(Copyright © by Nike, Inc./Wieder and Kennedy Reprinted with permission.)

"The only limit is the one you give yourself.
Don't settle for less than you can achieve.
The only way to find that out is to keep raising your bar,
you must just keep going, keep wanting more, no matter what."

-David Lessard, my dad and my very first hero

MY FIRST REAL RUN:
TO AND FOR MY LATE MOM

It was early afternoon on a fresh spring day in May 1995. I was keeping with my daily recovery routine after my lung transplant-taking pills, eating well, using the treadmill, lifting weights, making my goal list, and planning my new life-when it hit me.

I need to run! Like a lightning bolt, the desire coursed through my entire body as my heart started to beat faster and my lungs started to inhale and exhale a little more air with each breath. As I raced up the stairs to put on the new running outfit my parents had given me for Christmas, I grabbed the phone. "Dad, I'm running to Ma's." After a long pause he sighed and said, "OK, be careful." He knew me well enough not to question me.

My mother had gotten her wish to live long enough to see me get my lungs, but only for a short while. Five short months after my transplant, my mom died of cancer. She had always taken such good care of me. When her sickness wouldn't allow her to do that anymore, I think she felt she could take better care of me from Heaven. She knew it was killing me to watch her suffer when I had been given another chance at life.

"This first run is for her," I thought as I smiled and pulled out a crumpled piece of paper I had looked at many times. It was one of the last notes my mom had written me when she and I both were struggling to live. My dad had brought it over to my apartment during our "mail sessions." Occasionally the threat of infection to either one of us prevented us from seeing each other in person. At those times my mother and I communicated through notes.

The note I held in my hand was scribbled in my mom's shaky handwriting and simply said, "You run honey." I tried to breathe it in as I focused on hearing her voice saying these three words. I smiled, made the sign of the cross, and sent a kiss to her and God as I began my run, a goal I had waited for my whole life.

I had an excited bounce to my step, like Tigger from Winnie the Pooh, as I hopped down the stairs and onto the porch. For the fun of it, I checked out the bottom of my Nikes. I would look again after I was finished running, for proof that I had actually ran and begun to wear out the treads.

"Too bad they aren't Nike waffle trainers," I thought. I yearned to wear off the dots that sat upon the waffle squares. (The Nike waffle trainer was the first Nike shoe. An actual waffle iron was used to produce the first prototypes of the sole in 1974). That's OK. I would wear out whatever treads my Nikes had on them from now on. I told myself that one day maybe I'd have my own signature Nike line. Setting goals is a lifelong process. When you are starting to make new ones, make sure you grab hold of them and give them energy.

I started to run for the first time with my new lungs. I made a mental note to not go too fast too soon. I was determined to make it to the cemetery without stopping. I couldn't contain myself at first, galloping like a gazelle, watching the grass spread underneath, landing my feet on the pavement, and moving across the earth swiftly with lungs that were actually working. What joy I felt at this moment.

I was amazed at the feeling of breathing deeply without sharp pain or the need to stop. "Take it slow, Dottie," I thought. "Enjoy every second and move your feet and breathe. Just do it." I smiled with amazement.

A little girl in a passing car watched me as I ran. It reminded me of all the times I sat in the car with my nose pressed against the window yearning to be that runner. Here I was! Life doesn't get any better than this! Slowly I put one foot in front of the other, I took one breath at a time lumbering up a tiny hill, then onto a flat sidewalk toward my destination.

My legs were moving, and I watched the quick glimpse of the white swoosh on my Nikes go by me each time one foot passed the other. "We're doing it," I said to the Nikes. The swoosh that brought me through so much was now finally getting to fly.

After about a mile, I was happy for a slight downhill, as my breathing was getting a little stressed and my legs a bit tired. It was hard work, and I wanted to stop and rest for a little, but I was determined to keep moving.

I had to do this for my mother, and I started to focus on her and the fact that she was going to be the very first one to see me run. I looked down at the cracks in the cement and watched them go by swiftly to take my mind off the burning in my legs. I celebrated each breath. My breath was short because I was moving like an athlete not because I was sick and my lungs didn't work.

Wow, so this is how great it feels…very cool! I am a runner, I am an athlete. At that moment, everything I had gone through was worth it.

I rounded the corner and started down the street, where my mom, in spirit, was waiting at the bottom of the hill. "I'm coming, Mom," I said under my labored breathing. "I'm almost there," I said to myself and my new lungs, "You can't stop now."

I looked up and saw the entrance to the cemetery. I started to sprint. "I'm here, Mom! I'm running to you!" I exclaimed loudly, not caring if anyone heard me. I lifted my right arm up in triumph, now gasping for breath. I had no control over the feet that carried me as if they had wings to my mother's grave.

I started laughing with pure joy and childish excitement between gasps and tears. I collapsed over her headstone, allowing it to hold up my shaky body as I struggled to breathe. "We did it, Mom," I said, as I rested my head on the headstone as if it were her shoulder. "This was for you, you are the first one to get to see me run."

I was proud of myself for running but even more proud because I shared this gift with my mom. I stayed with her for a few minutes and then knelt into the damp dirt to thank her and God. I kissed her headstone and blew a kiss to Heaven. I know it landed directly on my mom's cheek. I could feel Joey and Penny smiling. They had run with me.

With tired legs I headed up the hill I had just sprinted down but with a sense of pride that I had never experienced before. I looked back once more as I got to the top of the hill and blew a kiss with a little wave. "See you next run, Mom." I headed home eager to tell my dad all about it.

"The difference between goal setting and goal getting is in knowing how to take the first step once you've decided what it is that you want."

- Gift from my own gift and coach Ben Brownsberger

My second run was to that rusty old fence at my grade school. I lined up on the white line just as I had done as a little girl. I yelled "go" and took off. I ran my heart out toward the fence and rejoiced with every step, thinking of all that I had gone through to relive this feeling that I had clung to so fiercely. I laughed as I slammed into the fence as hard as I could, with strength I had never had before. "I told you I'd be back," I laughed. "See you next time." For I now knew there would be many "next times."

MY FIRST "OFFICIAL" RACE: I AM AN A-T-H-L-E-T-E

The summer after my lung transplant my dad brought me an article from our local newspaper. "It's about a woman who competes in a sporting event as a transplant athlete," he said as he handed me the paper.

As I scanned the article, I was drawn to a picture of this woman, Vanessa Underwood. As I read her story, I felt goose bumps.

It was as if the curtains had been drawn and sunshine streamed in through the window and enveloped me with a warm peace. Her story reaffirmed what I always believed, that I really could become an athlete.

Vanessa had received two kidney transplants, and her story of survival and determination was amazing. However, I was more focused on the fact that the paper referred to her as an athlete.

One night I answered the phone and the voice on the other end said, "Hello Dottie, Ms. Double Lung Transplant, this is Vanessa, Double Kidney Transplant. You need to go to the transplant games." She had found out about me through a cousin.

The universe was indeed conspiring in my favor. We spoke for a long while, each of us expressing our excitement about life, being active, and having so many similar experiences. We knew almost immediately that we were one and the same.

Vanessa told me all about the National Kidney Foundation U.S. Transplant Games, an athletic event that calls attention to the success of organ and tissue transplantation. The games started in 1982 with just a few hundred athletes. By 1994, the year I received my new lungs, it had already grown to more than 1,000 participants. Vanessa convinced me to start training for the next games in 1996.

The thought of competing against other people was exciting and scary at the same time. To ease my fears, Vanessa brought me to a meeting for the games. I met people with heart, liver, and kidney transplants. I was the first athlete on my team with a lung transplant, which was extremely exciting.

I started to train for my first real race. It was fun and funny at the same time, because I had no idea what I was doing.

For years, I had watched sprinters on television, seeing them focus like animals in pursuit of prey. I never paid much attention to their technical form or how they used strategy. I just watched them run fast. I wasn't watching how they maneuvered around the track, planning and plotting their every move. I wasn't even aware that you are supposed to stay in your lane until my father told me one day when I was at the track practicing. At the age of 29, I was a virgin athlete.

When we arrived at the games, I looked around in awe and with great pride, these people were just like me! I felt a bit unprepared but ready for the challenge and ready to "just do it." As I stood in the registration line, I felt so proud that I had made it to this place in my life, a place I had always dreamed of.

This was my Olympics. My dream was becoming a reality. As I checked in, I was handed an event gym bag given only to athletes. I opened it with curiosity and excitement.

The first thing my hand grasped was a green identification tag that read "Dottie Lessard, ATHLETE." I couldn't believe my eyes. I placed the tag around my neck and felt it lay atop my chest. I was home, and I felt like the luckiest girl alive.

I still have that green tag. It is more important to me than any medals I've won; it is my greatest trophy.

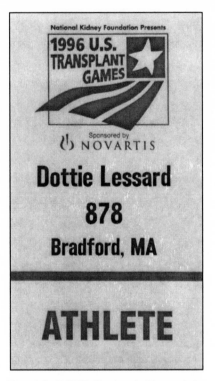

National Kidney Foundation Presents

**1996 U.S.
TRANSPLANT
GAMES**

Sponsored by
℧ NOVARTIS

Dottie Lessard
878
Bradford, MA

ATHLETE

(Copyright © 1996. Reprinted with permission
from the National Kidney Foundation, Inc.)

This was the badge of honor that I had been training for my entire life. I wore something that identified me as an athlete, me, the girl who wasn't supposed to ever grow up, never mind run. Yeah, the same girl everyone told "no" and called a dreamer had officially become an "ATHLETE."

"Wow Dottie, you really did it," I thought as I let those seven little letters, A-T-H-L-E-T-E, soak into my heart and soul.

MY FIRST RACE: A FOURTH-PLACE TRIUMPH

The night before the transplant games, I attended an Olympic-style opening ceremony. A torch was lit and the song *I Will Remember You* played as the faces of our "angels," our heroes, the organ donors, flashed upon a stadium screen. It was emotional and strengthening to the core.

The next day was my race, the 100-meter sprint. My dad was in the stands, and it was comforting to glance up and see him there proud as can be. This was his day as much as it was mine, and I knew that somehow my mom was there as well.

This was my first real race and I didn't have a clue what to expect. I looked around at the other women standing next to me and wondered what it would be like to run beside them.

For a brief magical moment, I was that first-grader ready to bang into the rusty fence. My heart was pounding, and my lungs were working strongly as I focused on trying to take some deep breaths in and out for assurance. I was in the third lane and looked right down the middle of it, making a mental note to not step anywhere near the white lines as my dad had warned. The nervous energy, the excitement, it all felt good.

An official came by and asked me if I wanted him to set up my starting block. I politely said, "No thanks," and vowed to figure out how to use that weird looking thing before my next race.

The gun fired, and off I went. I could hear my dad's words ringing in my ears, "stay in your lane!" It took the first few steps for me to realize I was actually running in a race and even passing some of the other women.

Near the end, I was so overwhelmed that I started to slow down. I had been in third place, but I was passed within the last few yards to take fourth.

I didn't really care, because I realized I had just done what I had dreamed of doing my entire life. When I looked up at the stands to see my dad, he was shaking his head laughing.

Afterward he told me, "You're supposed to run through the finish. Not slow down!" That was something I had to learn: How to be a runner. Now I never forget to run hard and fast way past the finish line.

After the race I congratulated everyone, especially the runners who ran faster than me. I studied the joy on their faces and breathed it into my new lungs for memory. I gave them all hugs, and we all celebrated and captured the moment by taking pictures.

I gathered my belongings, and my dad and I headed off the track and across the grassy field. I could tell he was happy and proud of me because I saw it in his eyes. I had just run a race that he had heard me pray for my entire life. A race he may have thought I would never truly run.

I am sure he would never admit it, but with the odds my parents were given, the statistics about my survival, and all the risks of surgery, I am sure he had his doubts. That race changed his life forever as well.

As I threw my spikes over my shoulder like a veteran, I laced my arm through his and said, "We got our race dad and one day we will have a gold medal to go with it." He smiled and said "Oh Dot. We'll see." For one of the first times in both our lives, we were excited for what the future would hold.

It was an amazing day I will never forget. I accomplished my goal few believed would ever happen. I was officially an athlete.

I did go on to win "our gold" four years later in the 100-meter sprint at the transplant games. The races and medals that would follow became so much more to me than running and winning. Everyone at those games was my teammate in the Game of Life.

Getting second (or third) chances in life can give you an exhilarated spirit and gifts as well. We all have things we are grateful for and when we are we produce feelings of appreciation, positive vibrations that allow us to feel good inside. That feeling from inside spreads to others when we share our gifts.

LIVING MY DREAM AND FINDING A GIFT: INSPIRING OTHERS THROUGH COMPETITION

It isn't just being an athlete that makes me proud. It is what I can do as an athlete and who I can reach while doing it that really matters.

When I'm at the games, I take every chance I can to see little kids who have received transplants. They come in all shapes and all sizes with all kinds of horror stories about their illnesses, the operations they endured, and the loss of friends with the same diseases.

I received one of my biggest gifts from one of these little heroes after running the 100-meter sprint at the 2000 Transplant Olympic games.

There I was waiting for the starting gun. My fingers twitching with untamed excitement. My arms set to propel me forward. I hated and loved that moment at the same time. It was nerve-wracking and thrilling, pure life. I live for that split second after the gun explodes, when you burst from the start as excited as a little kid on Christmas morning. It doesn't get old or less exciting.

I felt strong coming down my lane, and I ran hard, straight through the finish. I won! I couldn't believe it. As I scanned the stands for my father, I suddenly felt something hard plow into me.

I looked down and there was this white shirt and little arms clinging to my thighs. A small head pressed against my stomach. I reached down and pulled up the cutest little boy I had ever seen. He wrapped his arms around my neck like an octopus, and I folded my arms around him just as tightly. What an amazing embrace it was.

Within seconds his mom was standing next to us, with a smile and a light of joy I cannot explain. I caught her gaze, but I was still in my own world with this amazing little boy clinging to me. He didn't want to get down or let go. "I'm so sorry," the mother apologized. "He just bolted out of my arms when he saw you win."

"Congratulations," she continued, "that was amazing!" I smiled as I managed to pry my arm loose in order to shake her hand. He still kept a tight hold around my neck, and I didn't let go either. Finally, Cullen, a four-year-old who had received a liver transplant at age two, decided to climb down and settle for holding my hand. We walked on the sidelines back toward the stands.

Cullen's mom said she had never seen him act like that before. "It's our first games. You're his new hero," she gushed. I felt as if I had just won the lottery. My first gold medal for running suddenly didn't matter. I was now a hero to someone who needed to know that dreams do come true. He had seen his hopes in me even at four years old. A light bulb went off for me that day. My reason for becoming an athlete was not just for my own sake but also to inspire others.

I do what I do because it is my purpose and I love it. I also do it to inspire kids to never give up on their dreams. My desire is that all children will have a future, one that they create despite all their obstacles.

*If I didn't always set goals for myself I truly believe I would
not be here today. Everyone needs goals in their life.
Something to reach for, strive for, and to hold onto and grasp.
The feeling of accomplishment when you reach a goal will
propel you forward to strive for your next one.*

I had become an athlete. Nothing would stop me from running as many days as I could. Whenever or wherever I wanted. That is until my kidneys began to fail. I guess God wanted me to overcome another obstacle to remind me of how precious the gift of life is. I felt my purpose was even bigger now.

After I received my kidney transplant, I became an athlete again. A professional Nike athlete.

I set the bar high to beat CF and survive a double lung transplant. I became an athlete. I had to re-set the bar to another, higher level to survive a kidney transplant. I survived both and not only became an athlete but I became a professional athlete. I became a Nike girl. Just like the one I had drawn in 1993.

Now I can run and slam into that rusty old fence anytime I want. Can you make it to that fence with me? Want to race? Do you think you can beat me?

YOUR TURN:

What are your seven letters?

Close this book for a moment. Take a look at the rusty fence on the cover.

Think about what the fences are in your life. Are your fences old, rusty, and shaky? Or are they new, strong, and topped with barbed wire? Are your fences real or are they imaginary? Do your fences keep you locked in? Or do your fences keep you locked out? Or are they really a beacon instead of a barrier?

Can you make it to your fences? Can you take one more breath or one more step and reach your fences no matter how bad things seem? When you understand what your fences are can you climb over, tunnel underneath, or just blast through them? Of course you can!

The seven letters that saved my life were A-T-H-L-E-T-E. They were my letters that motivated me to survive. Yours are sure to be different.

If you had to write down seven letters to save your life, what would they be? What word would they spell? If you can't think of seven letters, use a number that has significance to you. Write your letters down, right here, right now. Then create your own principles to go with them.

Attach a short-term and long-term action step to each of your letters. Write down at least one action step you could achieve within one week. Write down another you will strive to attain sometime within the next month or year.

Set an action step every day and carry it around with you. It can be something simple, like a vow to take the stairs instead of the elevator. Look at it throughout the day and recite it several times an hour. Re-program your thought patterns. Visualize and give feelings and emotions to what you want.

Look at and revise your goal lists often. Don't allow yourself to get discouraged if you haven't reached one in the time you gave yourself. Think of the goal you did reach and keep reaching. Keep taking action toward them and they will be achieved!

E - Encourage yourself and others to do great things

MY OWN SEVEN LETTERS:

1.

2.

3.

4.

5.

6.

7.

MY SEVEN SHORT TERM AND LONG TERM
ACTION STEPS FOR EACH LETTER:

1.

2.

3.

4.

5.

6.

7.

EPILOGUE

"Too often we are scared. Scared of what we might not be able to do. Scared of what people might think if we tried. We let our fears stand in the way of our hopes. We say no when we want to say yes. We sit quietly when we want to scream. And we shout with the others, when we should keep our mouths shut. Why? After all, we do only go around once. There's really no time to be afraid. So stop. Try something you've never tried. Risk it. Enter a triathlon. Write a letter to the editor. Demand a raise. Call winners at the toughest court. Throw away your television. Bicycle across the United States. Try bobsledding. Try anything. Speak out against the designated hitter. Travel to a country where you don't speak the language. Patent something. You have nothing to lose and everything to gain. JUST DO IT."

–Nike

(Copyright © by Nike, Inc./Wieder and Kennedy Reprinted with permission.)

They say that with every door that closes another one opens. Although I have started to walk through the new door, I have certainly just begun. My purpose will be to live as long and as fully as I can for my son, Liam, and to do whatever else my higher power has in store for me.

What is next for me? How am I going to raise my bar? Well, I am working on getting stronger by combining traditional medicine with alternative treatments. I continue to be a trailblazer having passed the 15 year mark of living with my lung transplant. I am determined to protect these gifts I've received from others by finding a balance between taking my daily immunosuppressant medication, living an active and healthy lifestyle and staying informed.

I continue my involvement as an athlete, coach, and mentor for the National Kidney Foundation, U.S. and World Transplant Olympics. I continue to empower others to run, jump, climb or leap. I celebrate every moment by living life to the fullest. I laugh and play with my son, Liam, tuck him into bed, hold his hand, and hear him say "Momma." I am going to tell my story in person to his children.

Always remember that anything is possible if you just believe and take action and move toward it. Always remember that you were chosen to be you and that you are worthy of great things and amazing love. Only you have the power to make things happen and change your outcome.

Your life is your gift to yourself and the world-when you give, you will indeed receive. Give to yourself and give to others.

If you are having trouble getting started, use the fact that you have read this far and are finishing my book as your first accomplishment.

Now go back through the pages and complete all the exercises. If you do, you will gain strength, encouragement, and the ability to accomplish your unique purpose in this lifetime. Continue to find ways to nourish it so that you soar.

I believe in you and now it's time for you to believe in yourself, more than you ever have. This present moment is all we have to live in. The past is gone. The future may never arrive. Be determined and be fearless, NOW and LIVE LIFE FULLY!

Yours in Faith,
Dottie

CF IS BEING TREATED

———————

Living with CF is far more possible now than it was when I was born in 1966. I truly believe a cure is just around the corner. We have so much hope.

More knowledge and advanced research, new medications, new treatments, and a better plan to treat and understand our lungs and the disease are happening every single day. It is my goal that kids can live with their own lungs forever and not have to get new ones or go to Heaven way too soon.

The CF Foundation and the Joey Fund (in memory of my dear friend Joey) are two places where you can find hope, inspiration, and many ways to assist us on this mission to keep every child with CF living and breathing freely until this disease becomes just a memory.

I personally thank you for helping in any way possible.

For more information please visit online:

cff.org
joeyfund.org

ORGAN DONATION

You would not be reading this story if two people had not unselfishly signed an organ donor card. However, being an organ donor is a personal decision. Only you can decide if it is right for you.

If you do wish to become an organ and/or tissue donor review the organ donor laws in the state you live in. Then you can complete one or more of the following: (1) Designate your decision to be an organ donor on your state driver's license; (2) Sign a donor card if you don't have a driver's license or one is required by your state; (3) Inform your family and your medical professional about your donation decision and your intentions; and/or (4) Register with your state donor registry.

For more information please visit online:

unos.org
kidney.org

ABOUT THE AUTHOR

Dottie Lessard is a two-time organ transplant recipient who received new lungs and a new kidney. She is a mother, writer, personal empowerment coach, motivational speaker, and a professional athlete from Boston.

Her amazing story has been featured many times on the radio, television, including HBO and in many different magazines and newspapers, including *Runner's World*, *USA Today*, the *Boston Herald*, and others.

As a personal empowerment coach, Dottie provides telephone and in-person coaching sessions.

As an experienced motivational and keynote speaker Dottie speaks to small and large audiences about finding hope and inspiration in her story, so their own hopes and dreams become attainable, no matter what their current circumstances may be.

As a professional athlete currently under contract with Nike, Dottie competes in, attends, and promotes many different athletic events across the country.

Dottie lives with her son, Liam, in her hometown just outside Boston, Massachusetts.

Visit Dottie online: dottielessard.com

ABOUT COCONUT AVENUE, INC.

Coconut Avenue, Inc. is a new publishing company founded by Stephen Lesavich, Ph.D., J.D. in 2008. Dr. Lesavich is a professional software engineer and technology expert with a Ph.D. in computer science and an attorney actively practicing intellectual property and technology law. He is considered by many to be a soul-growth visionary and pioneer.

Located on LaSalle Street, the heartbeat and pulse of the city of Chicago, Coconut Avenue publishes creative works with positive messages that promote soul-growth, personal empowerment and self-help that raise the collective vibration of our planet.

FOR MORE INFORMATION ABOUT OTHER COCONUT AVENUE® AUTHORS, BOOKS, PRODUCTS, AND EVENTS, PLEASE CONTACT:

Coconut Avenue, Inc.
39 S. LaSalle Street, Suite 325
Chicago, Illinois 60603 USA
312.419.9445 (v)
312.419.9446 (f)

e-mail: info@coconutavenue.com

On-line: coconutavenue.com

Coconut Avenue®
The Creative Avenue for Best Selling Authors®

Coconut Avenue,® *The Creative Avenue For Best Selling Authors*®
and the *Coconut Avenue graphic,*® are registered U.S. Trademarks
of Coconut Avenue, Inc.

CPSIA information can be obtained at www.ICGtesting.com
Printed in the USA
LVOW050024240812

295615LV00001B/95/P

9 780980 104035